Checking the key features of a fungus –

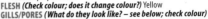

Plums and Custard
Tricholomopsis rutilans (inedible)

HABITA
it n
OCCURI

CAP *(Cl*
con
red
STEM *(*
fragi
reddish-purple scales
FLESH *(Check colour; does it change colour?)* Yellow
GILLS/PORES *(What do they look like? – see below; check colour)*
Narrowly attached to stem; custard yellow
SPORES *(The spores can colour grass and leaves below the cap; or place a cap on a sheet of paper, leave for a few hours, spores will drop from the gills and colour the paper below)* White
SMELL *(Does it have a smell?)* Smells like rotting wood

Similar species – it is important that all the features check out when identifying a fungus, as some very poisonous fungi can, at first glance, look almost the same as an edible species, such as the examples below. **Remember, never eat a fungus unless you are quite sure that you have identified it correctly.**

Wood Mushroom (edible)

Deathcap (deadly poisonous)

Check underneath the cap – most fungi have gills attached to the underside of the cap, but some, mainly boletes (pages 50–55) and some bracket fungi (pages 62–65), have tubes which look like spongy pores. The colour of the gills/pores can change once the spores have dropped, or they may bruise a different colour, or exude a liquid.

Milkcap species exude a milky liquid

Gills

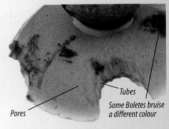

Pores

Tubes

Some Boletes bruise a different colour

How are the gills attached to the stem? – The way the gills are attached to the stem can differ, and can be an important identification feature.

Free of stem (described as **free** in most guides)

Narrowly attached to stem (described as **adnexed** in most guides)

Broadly attached to stem (described as **adnate** in most guides)

Running down onto stem (described as **decurrent** in most guides)

Not all fungi have gills and pores, and they come in a variety of shapes – not always the traditional toadstool shape.

Fungi can be found in a wide variety of habitats, appearing on the ground in grass and leaf litter, or on living and dead wood. Some may favour a particular habitat or are found exclusively with one type of tree. The main habitats, and some of the best places to look locally, are described here.

Grassland and heathland

The chalk and limestone grassland of the Chilterns, Cotswolds and the Downs, the unimproved meadows in the Thames Vale and the Berkshire heathlands are not as rich in fungi as the woodlands, but there are several groups of fungi that favour these habitats, especially the waxcaps (see pages 8–11).

LOOK FOR Waxcaps (pictured), Fool's Funnel, Field Blewit, Flowery Blewit, The Miller, pinkgills, Parasol, Field Mushroom, Horse Mushroom, Shaggy Inkcap, Snowy Inkcap, mottlegills, Liberty Cap, Lurid Bolete, Golden Spindles, Meadow Coral, Moor Club, puffballs

Broadleaved woodland

Broadleaved woodland is by far the richest habitat for fungi. The diversity of tree species in a woodland can increase the number of fungi found there, as many fungi favour certain tree species. Oak, birch and beech are all worth looking under, or on.

OAK – LOOK FOR Spindle Toughshank, Clustered Bonnet, Deceiving Knight, Sulphur Knight, Deathcap, Oakbug Milkcap, Yellowdrop Milkcap, Watery Milkcap, Dark Cep, Inkstain Bolete (pictured), Ruby Bolete, Gilded Bolete

BIRCH – LOOK FOR Birch Knight, Fly Agaric, Orange Grisette, Tawny Grisette, Birch Webcap, Pearly Webcap, Woolly Milkcap, Bearded Milkcap, Grey Milkcap, Ugly Milkcap, Green Brittlegill, Yellow Swamp Brittlegill, Orange Birch Bolete, Brown Birch Bolete, Mottled Bolete, Brown Rollrim, Birch Polypore

BEECH – LOOK FOR Ivory Woodwax, Pearly Parachute, Porcelain Fungus, Saffrondrop Bonnet, Burnt Knight, False Deathcap, Magpie Inkcap (pictured), Purple Stocking Webcap, Yellow Webcap, Beech Milkcap, Beechwood Sickener, Greencracked Brittlegill, Geranium Brittlegill, Bitter Beech Bolete, Old Man of the Woods, Horn of Plenty, Oyster Mushroom

MIXED – LOOK FOR Clouded Funnel, Butter Cap, Amethyst Deceiver, Wood Blewit, Skullcap Dapperling, Shaggy Parasol, Wood Mushroom, Shaggy Scalycap, Bruising Webcap, Charcoal Burner, Cep, White Saddle

3

Coniferous woodland

Many species of fungi favour, or are only found in, conifer plantations, or with planted conifers within broadleaved woodland. Bernwood Forest (Bucks) has a rich diversity of fungi under the conifers, especially amongst the carpet of moss.

LOOK FOR Spotted Toughshank, Plums and Custard, Liver Milkcap, The Sickener, False Saffron Milkcap, Bloody Brittlegill, Fruity Brittlegill (pictured), Primrose Brittlegill, Slippery Jack, Bovine Bolete, Weeping Bolete, False Chanterelle, Yellow Stagshorn

Berkshire sites

Although Berkshire is a small county there are many good fungus-hunting areas, particularly around Newbury in the west of the county and from Windsor Great Park to the heath and plantation areas south of Wokingham and Bracknell.

PLACES TO VISIT Bucklebury Common (2 miles north of Newbury), **Snelsmore Common Country Park** (2 miles north of Newbury), **Bowdown Woods Nature Reserve** (2½ miles south-east of Newbury), **Greenham Common** (2½ miles south-east of Newbury), **Moor Copse Nature Reserve** (5 miles west of Reading), **Windsor Great Park** (2 miles south of Windsor), **California Country Park** (2½ miles south-west of Wokingham), **Wildmoor Heath Nature Reserve** (1 mile north of Sandhurst). Visit www.bbowt.org.uk for more information on the nature reserves listed.

LOOK FOR Snowy Waxcap, Crimson Waxcap, Cedarwood Waxcap, The Deceiver, Wood Blewit, Field Blewit, Sulphur Knight (pictured right), Fly Agaric, Snakeskin Grisette, Tawny Grisette (pictured above), Skullcap Dapperling, Green Dapperling, Shaggy Scalycap, Yellow Webcap, Bloodred Webcap, Lilac Fibrecap, Grey Milkcap, Ochre Brittlegill, Purple Brittlegill, Inkstain Bolete, Bitter Beech Bolete, Orange Birch Bolete, Chanterelle, Moor Club, Pipe Club, Jellybaby

4

Buckinghamshire sites

Buckinghamshire has many fine woodlands on the clay vale, running diagonally from Milton Keynes down to the exceptionally fungus-rich Bernwood Forest near the Oxfordshire border. The Buckinghamshire Chilterns, in the south of the county, with their chalk grasslands and beech woodlands have some of the best areas to visit (see Sites in the Chiltern Hills).

PLACES TO VISIT Little Linford Wood Nature Reserve (4½ miles north of Milton Keynes), **Finemere Wood Nature Reserve** (8 miles north-west of Aylesbury), **Rushbeds Wood Nature Reserve** (9 miles south-east of Bicester), **Whitecross Green Wood Nature Reserve** (5 miles south of Bicester), **Bernwood Forest** (7 miles north-east of Oxford). Visit www.bbowt.org.uk for more information on the nature reserves listed.

LOOK FOR Aniseed Funnel, Butter Cap, Branched Shanklet, Amethyst Deceiver, Wood Blewit, Rosy Bonnet, Birch Knight, Plums and Custard, Deathcap, Fly Agaric, Parasol, Bruising Webcap, Birch Webcap, Orange Milkcap, Yellowdrop Milkcap, Fruity Brittlegill, Charcoal Burner (pictured above), Cep, Inkstain Bolete, Gilded Bolete, Brown Birch Bolete, Trumpet Chanterelle, Wood Hedgehog, Yellow Club, Yellow Stagshorn (pictured right), Earthfan, Conifer Blueing Bracket, Stinkhorn

Oxfordshire sites

Oxfordshire has many interesting areas for fungi from the Cotswolds in the west to the limestone grasslands and woodlands around Oxford and Abingdon. The Oxfordshire Chilterns, in the south of the county, with their chalk grasslands and beech woodlands have some of the best areas to visit (see Sites in the Chiltern Hills).

PLACES TO VISIT Foxholes Nature Reserve (4 miles north of Burford), **Wychwood Forest** (2 miles west of Charlbury), **Sydlings Copse Nature Reserve** (3½ miles north-east of Oxford), **Shotover Country Park** (2 miles east of Oxford), **Dry Sandford Pit Nature Reserve** (2½ miles south-west of Abingdon), **Lashford Lane Fen Nature Reserve** (4 miles south-west of Oxford). Visit www.bbowt.org.uk for more information on the nature reserves listed.

LOOK FOR Meadow Waxcap, Blackening Waxcap, Parrot Waxcap, Pink Waxcap, Clouded Funnel, Fool's Funnel, Wood Blewit, Porcelain Fungus, Rosy Bonnet (pictured right), Soapy Knight, Sulphur Knight, False Deathcap, Dearthcap, Fly Agaric, Indigo Pinkgill, Mousepee Pinkgill (pictured above), Lilac Dapperling, Parasol, Fairy Inkcap, Pearly Webcap, Woolly Milkcap, Watery Milkcap, Beechwood Sickener, Bay Bolete, Scarletina Bolete, Lurid Bolete, Parasitic Bolete, Chicken of the Woods, Common Earthball, Scarlet Elfcup

Sites in the Chiltern Hills

The Chiltern Hills with their dramatic escarpment, beechwoods and hidden valleys, run diagonally from the Bedfordshire border in a south-westerly direction across the southern half of Buckinghamshie and Oxfordshire to the River Thames at Goring. They are still heavily wooded and have some of the best areas to seach for fungi.

PLACES TO VISIT Dancersend Nature Reserve (5 miles south-east of Aylesbury), **Wendover Woods** (4½ miles south-east of Aylesbury), **Pulpit Hill** (2 miles north-east of Princes Risborough), **Millfield Wood Nature Reserve** (1½ miles north of High Wycombe), **Aston Rowant National Nature Reserve** (2 miles south of Chinnor), **Warburg Nature Reserve** (4 miles north-west of Henley-on-Thames), **Lambridge Woods** (3 miles north-west of Henley-on-Thames). Visit www.bbowt.org.uk for more information on the nature reserves listed.

LOOK FOR Ivory Woodwax, Amethyst Deceiver, Pearly Parachute, Porcelain Fungus, Saffrondrop Bonnet, False Deathcap, Freckled Dapperling, Magpie Inkcap, Verdigris Agaric (pictured above), Purple Stocking Webcap, Beech Milkcap, Beechwood Sickener, Geranium Brittlegill, Red Cracking Bolete, Old Man of the Woods, Horn of Plenty, Oyster Mushroom, Collared Earthstar (pictured right)

The fungi described in this section can all be found locally and have been chosen because of their distinctive features. Many are common, some less often seen. They may be restricted to a particular habitat or associated with just one type of tree. Similar species are also mentioned.

Trumpet Chanterelle –
Cantherellus tubaeformis

Ivory Woodwax
Hygrophorus eburneus (inedible)

HABITAT Amongst leaf litter in broadleaved woodland, especially with beech
OCCURRENCE Autumn; occasional

CAP 3–7cm across; convex then flattened; slimy; white
STEM 4–7cm long x 5–10mm thick; slimy, tapering towards base; white
FLESH White, thick in cap
GILLS Running down onto stem; white
SPORES White
SMELL Faintly fruity, like mandarin peel

7

Herald of Winter
Hygrophorus hypothejus (inedible)

HABITAT With pine trees
OCCURRENCE Late autumn–winter; occasional

CAP 3–6cm across; convex then flattening, often with a central depression; slimy; olive brown, paler along the edge
STEM 4–7cm long x 7–14mm thick; slimy; whitish, tinged yellow-orange
FLESH Whitish to yellow, bruising orange
GILLS Running down onto stem; pale yellow
SPORES White
SMELL Not distinctive

Meadow Waxcap
Hygrocybe pratensis (edible)

HABITAT Grassland, occasionally in scrub
OCCURRENCE Autumn; common

CAP 3–8cm across, convex then flattened with a broad, central
hump; buff to orange-brown
STEM 2–5cm long x 10–15mm thick; tapering towards base;
whitish-buff to pale orange-brown
FLESH Thick in cap; pale buff
GILLS Running down onto stem, widely spaced; pale buff
SPORES White
SMELL Mushroomy

SIMILAR SPECIES

Toasted Waxcap *Hygrocybe colemanniana*
(edible), a rare species, found in grassland
on chalk or limestone, is similar in size, but
pinkish-brown with a darker brown centre
(as if toasted). The gills, often crinked and
interveined, run down onto the stem.

8

Blackening Waxcap
Hygrocybe conica (**poisonous**)

HABITAT Grassland, lawns, occasionally in open woodland
OCCURRENCE Autumn–early winter; common

CAP 3.5–5.5cm across; conical, splitting radially; orange to red,
blackening with age
STEM 3–7cm long x 6–10mm thick; yellow to scarlet with
white base, blackening with age
FLESH Yellow in cap, white in stem, blackening
GILLS Narrowly attached to stem or free of stem; pale yellow
SPORES White
SMELL Not distinctive

SIMILAR SPECIES

Scarlet Waxcap *Hygrocybe coccinea* (edible)
is similar in size, has a bright scarlet, convex
to flat cap. **Crimson Waxcap** *Hygrocybe
punicee* (edible) is larger and has a blood-red
cap (see page 9). These and several smaller
red or orange-red waxcaps are also found in
grassland but do not blacken with age.

Parrot Waxcap
Hygrocybe psittacina (inedible)

HABITAT Grassland, lawns, heathland
OCCURRENCE Summer–winter; common

CAP 1–3cm across; bell-shaped or convex, slimy; greenish at first, then yellowish-green, sometimes with flesh tones
STEM 2–4cm long x 2–3mm thick; green, blue-green at top
FLESH White, tinged yellow-green
GILLS Broadly attached to stem; greenish with yellow edge
SPORES White
SMELL Mushroomy

SIMILAR SPECIES

Mousepee Pinkgill *Entoloma incanum* (**poisonous**), found in chalk/limestone grassland, is similar in size (see page 27). Cap is flatter, olive-green to yellow-brown with a darker dimple in centre; not slimy. Stem yellow-green bruising blue-green. Gills are greenish-white becoming pinkish. Smells strongly of mice.

Crimson Waxcap
Hygrocybe punicea (edible)

HABITAT Grassland, lawns, heathland
OCCURRENCE Autumn; occasional

CAP 5–12cm across; bell-shaped then flatter, often irregularly lobed; greasy; deep blood-red, fading to orange-red
STEM 5–12cm long x 6–20mm thick; covered in coarse fibres; yellow, flushed red, whitish towards the base
FLESH White, yellowish in cap
GILLS Narrowly attached to stem; yellowish, flushed orange-red
SPORES White
SMELL Not distinctive

SIMILAR SPECIES

Scarlet Waxcap *Hygrocybe coccinea* (edible), found in similar habitats, is much more common. It has a smaller (2–4cm across), bright scarlet, convex to flat cap, slimy at first. The flesh is yellow-red. Gills broadly attached to stem with a tooth, yellow, later red with a yellowish edge.

Pink Waxcap
Hygrocybe calyptriformis (inedible)

HABITAT Grassland, meadows
OCCURRENCE Late autumn–winter; uncommon

CAP 3–6cm across; conical, expanding and splitting radially – giving the impression of a ballerina's tutu (hence its other common name – Ballerina Waxcap); pink then whitish-pink
STEM 6–12cm long x 8–10mm thick; brittle; white, flushed pinkish-white at top
FLESH Pink in cap, white in stem
GILLS Free of stem, waxy; pale pink
SPORES White
SMELL Not distinctive

SIMILAR SPECIES

Other conical-capped **waxcap** *Hygrocybe* species are found in grassland, but none have the unmistakable delicate pink colour of the Pink Waxcap.

10

Golden Waxcap
Hygrocybe chlorophana (edible)

HABITAT Grassland, meadows, open broadleaved woodland
OCCURRENCE Late summer–winter; occasional

CAP 3–6cm across; convex to flat; very slimy when wet; bright yellow
STEM 3–6cm long x 6–8mm thick; yellow with white base
FLESH Pale yellow
GILLS Broadly attached to stem; pale yellow with a whitish edge
SPORES White
SMELL Not distinctive

SIMILAR SPECIES

Persistent Waxcap *Hygrocybe persistans* (inedible), similar in size, has a dry, yellow, irregularly lobed, conical cap. Found in grassland, summer. **Butter Waxcap** *Hygrocybe ceracea* (edible) has a smaller (1–2.5cm across) yellow, greasy cap, yellow gills running down or broadly attached to stem. Found in grassland, autumn–winter.

Snowy Waxcap
Hygrocybe virginea (edible)

HABITAT Grassland, lawns, occasionally in open woodland
OCCURRENCE Autumn–winter; common

CAP 1–5cm across, convex then flat; white, ivory to ochre later; smooth and slippery
STEM 2.5–5cm long x 2–4mm thick; solid and tapering towards base; white
FLESH White
GILLS Running down onto stem, widely spaced and waxy; white
SPORES White
SMELL Not distinctive

SIMILAR SPECIES

Cedarwood waxcap *Hygrocybe russocoriacea* (inedible), found in grassland and heathland, is smaller, but has a yellow-ivory convex cap (see below). Smells of sandalwood. Two **deadly poisonous** fungi of similar size, **Fool's Funnel** *Clitocybe rivulosa* (see page 13) and **Ivory Funnel** *Clitocybe dealbata*, are also found in grassland, usually forming small rings.

Cedarwood Waxcap
Hygrocybe russocoriacea (inedible)

HABITAT Grassland, lawns, heathland
OCCURRENCE Autumn; occasional

CAP 1–2cm across; convex; whitish to yellow-ivory, faintly edged with fine lines
STEM 2–3.5cm long x 2–3mm thick; slightly wavy, tapering towards base; whitish
FLESH Whitish
GILLS Running down onto stem; widely spaced; white
SPORES White
SMELL Perfumed, like sandalwood

SIMILAR SPECIES

Snowy Waxcap *Hygrocybe virginea* (edible), found in grassland, has a white cap, becoming more ochre with age (see above). Gills run onto stem. Smell not distinctive.

Honey Fungus
Armillaria mellea (edible when cooked)

HABITAT Parasitic, forming dense clusters on or around trunks
of broadleaved trees or conifers
OCCURRENCE Summer–early winter; very common

CAP 3–12cm across; convex then flattened and wavy;
variable in colour from ochre/tawny to dark brown
often with an olive tinge, covered in darker scales
STEM 6–15cm long x 5–15mm thick; yellowish
with reddish-brown base and a woolly
whitish-yellow ring
FLESH White
GILLS Running slightly down onto stem;
white then yellowish, later
pinkish-brown
SPORES Cream
SMELL Strong and mushroomy

SIMILAR SPECIES

Armillaria cepistipes is slightly
smaller and more yellow in
colour. **Dark Honey Fungus**
Armillaria ostoyae is more scaly
and has a brown-tinged ring.
Ringless Honey Fungus
Armillaria tabescens is smaller
and has no ring on stem.

Clouded Funnel
Clitocybe nebularis (inedible)

HABITAT Broadleaved and coniferous woodland, in troops or rings
OCCURRENCE Late summer–early winter; very common

CAP 5–20cm across; convex then flattened or slightly
depressed, edge of cap inrolled; cloudy grey, darker
in centre, sometimes with a buff tinge
STEM 5–10cm long x 15–25mm thick; swollen base,
fibrous becoming hollow; white to pale grey
FLESH White and thick
GILLS Running down onto stem; whitish,
later creamy-yellow
SPORES Cream
SMELL Strong and sweetish, slightly
unpleasant

SIMILAR SPECIES

Soapy Knight *Tricholoma
saponaceum* (inedible) is smaller
and is also found in broadleaved
and coniferous woodland,
forming troops but not rings
(see page 20). Cap is similar in
colour but often has olive or
rusty tints. Smells of soap.

Aniseed Funnel
Clitocybe odora (edible)

HABITAT In leaf litter in broadleaved and coniferous woodland, often in troops or rings
OCCURRENCE Autumn–early winter; common

CAP 3–8cm across; convex with a broad central hump, later expanding and becoming wavy; blue-green, greyish or greyish-green
STEM 3–6cm long x 5–10mm thick; flushed with cap colour
FLESH Whitish
GILLS Running slightly down onto stem; whitish tinged with cap colour
SPORES White
SMELL Strongly aniseed

SIMILAR SPECIES

Fragrant Funnel *Clitocybe fragrans* (inedible) also smells of aniseed, but is much smaller and is creamy-brown in colour. **Verdigris Agaric** *Stropharia aeruginosa* (inedible) also found in broadleaved and coniferous woodland, has a blue-green cap with a fleecy edge and grey-brown gills (see page 35).

Fool's Funnel
Clitocybe rivulosa (deadly poisonous)

HABITAT Grassland on sandy soil, in troops or rings
OCCURRENCE Late summer–autumn; common

CAP 2–5cm across; convex then flat and depressed in centre; powdery white, often with concentric rings where the buff-coloured flesh shows through
STEM 2–4cm long x 4–10mm thick; whitish
FLESH White to buff
GILLS Running down onto stem, crowded; white to buff
SPORES White
SMELL Sweet

SIMILAR SPECIES

The ring-forming **Ivory Funnel** *Clitocybe dealbata* (deadly poisonous) is similar in size and colour. **Snowy Waxcap** *Hygrocybe virginea* (edible) sometimes grows in troops (see page 11). Both are found in grassland. **The Miller** *Clitopilus prunulus* (edible), found in open woodland, has a whitish cap that feels like glove leather. Gills white becoming pink. Smells of flour.

Butter Cap
Collybia butyracea (inedible)

HABITAT In leaf litter, broadleaved and coniferous woodland
OCCURRENCE Late summer–early winter; very common

CAP 3–7cm across; convex then flat with a central hump; greasy like butter (hence the name); dark reddish-brown, drying pale tan to ivory
STEM 2.5–5cm long x 5–10mm thick; swollen towards base, tough and fibrous; reddish-brown, paler at top
FLESH Whitish-buff
GILLS Free of stem; whitish
SPORES White
SMELL Mushroomy to slightly rancid

SIMILAR SPECIES

Club Foot *Ampulloclitocybe clavipes* (inedible), found in broadleaved and coniferous woodland, is similar in size and with a stem swollen towards base. Cap, however, is paler and not greasy, and the gills, yellow-cream in colour, run down onto stem.

Spindle Toughshank
Collybia fusipes (inedible)

HABITAT In tufts at base of broadleaved trees, especially oak and beech
OCCURRENCE Early summer–early winter; common

CAP 3–7cm across; convex with broad central hump; dark red-brown
STEM 4–9cm long x 7–15mm thick; swollen in middle, tapering to thin rooting base, tough and fibrous; pale tan at top, red-brown towards base
FLESH Whitish-buff
GILLS Free of stem; whitish, then reddish-brown
SPORES White
SMELL Pleasant

SIMILAR SPECIES

Spectacular Rustgill *Gymnopilus junonius* (inedible) also grows in tufts at base of broadleaved trees, but is much larger and is a rich golden-brown, with rusty-coloured gills (see page 39). Several other species grow in tufts on wood, but do not have the distinctive fibrous, spindle-shaped stem.

Spotted Toughshank
Collybia maculata (inedible)

HABITAT In broadleaved and, especially coniferous woodland
OCCURRENCE Summer–autumn; very common

CAP 4–10cm across; flattened convex; white at first, later spotting and bruising rusty brown with age
STEM 5–10cm long x 8–12mm thick; sometimes rooting at base, tough and fibrous; white, discolouring rusty brown
FLESH White, bitter
GILLS Free of stem; white, becoming spotted rusty brown
SPORES Cream to pale pink
SMELL Not distinctive

SIMILAR SPECIES

Blue Spot Knight *Tricholoma columbetta* (edible), found in broadleaved and coniferous woodland, is similar in size. Cap is silky white and sometimes has pinkish, greenish or bluish spots when old.

Branched Shanklet
Collybia racemosa (inedible)

HABITAT Coniferous woodland, often amongst moss
OCCURRENCE Autumn; rare

CAP 0.5–1cm across; convex with a central hump; lead grey to greyish-brown
STEM 2–4cm long x 1–2mm thick; branched with tiny, capped outgrowths; lead grey to greyish-brown
FLESH Greyish
GILLS Free of stem; greyish
SPORES Whitish
SMELL Not distinctive

SIMILAR SPECIES

Although there are many tiny brownish fungi found amongst moss, there are no similar species – the distinctive stem of the Branched Shanklet is unmistakable.

Velvet Shank or Winter Fungus
Flammulina velutipes (edible)

HABITAT In clusters on rotting broadleaved trees
OCCURRENCE Late autumn–spring, can survive frozen in winter (hence its other common name – Winter Fungus); very common

CAP 2–10cm across; convex then flat; slimy; yellow-tan to orange-brown in centre
STEM 3–10cm long x 4–8mm thick; tough like gristle; dark brown and densely velvety, yellowish at top
FLESH Yellow-tan
GILLS Narrowly attached to stem; pale yellow
SPORES White
SMELL Pleasant

SIMILAR SPECIES

Sulphur Tuft *Hypholoma fasciculare* (**poisonous**) is similar in size, but has sulphur yellow gills which turn purple-brown as spores drop (see page 34). **Spectacular Rustgill** *Gymnopilus junonius* (inedible) is much larger and golden-brown, with rusty-coloured gills (see page 39).

16

Silky Piggyback
Asterophora parasitica (inedible)

HABITAT On rotting brittlegill *Russula* and milkcap *Lactarius* fungi, usually Blackening Brittlegill *Russula nigricans* (see page 49), in broadleaved and coniferous woodland
OCCURRENCE Summer–early winter; occasional

CAP 0.5–1.5cm across; convex to bell-shaped then flatter; silky, white, tinged greyish-lilac
STEM 1–3cm long x 1–3mm thick; white, often flushed brownish or greyish-lilac
FLESH Brown
GILLS Broadly attached to stem; grey
SPORES Pale brown
SMELL Not distinctive

SIMILAR SPECIES

Several small **parachute** *Marasmius* species, found on twigs and fallen leaves, look similar. **Powdery Piggyback** *Asterophora lycoperdoides* (inedible), found mainly on rotting Blackening Brittlegill *Russula nigricans*, is similar in size, but has a rounded, powdery, clay-brown cap.

The Deceiver
Laccaria laccata (edible)

HABITAT Mixed woodland and heathland
OCCURRENCE Late summer–early winter; very common

CAP 1.5–6cm across; convex then flat with a central
depression, becoming wavy and lined at the edge;
often scurfy; yellow-brown to brick-red when
moist, drying ochre to pale tan
STEM 5–10cm long x 6–10mm thick; rough, fibrous,
often twisted; yellow-brown to brick-red
FLESH Reddish-brown
GILLS Broadly attached to stem, widely spaced;
pinkish-salmon
SPORES White
SMELL Not distinctive

SIMILAR SPECIES

Scurfy Deceiver *Laccaria
proxima* (edible), found on
heathland and bogs, is very
similar in size and colour, but
scurfy cap not so wavy and stem
thicker towards the base.

Amethyst Deceiver
Laccaria amethystina (edible)

SIMILAR SPECIES

Lilac Fibrecap *Inocybe geophylla* var.
lilacina (**poisonous**), found in open areas
and paths in broadleaved and coniferous
woodland, is smaller, has a fibrous, pale
lilac-purple cap, lilac stem and clay-
coloured gills (see page 40).

HABITAT Broadleaved and coniferous woodland
OCCURRENCE Late summer–autumn; very common

CAP 1–6cm across; convex then flat or slightly depressed; deep
purple drying pale lilac-buff; centre sometimes tinged olive
STEM 4–10cm long x 5–10mm thick; becoming hollow; deep
purple with whitish fibres
FLESH Lilac
GILLS Broadly attached to stem, widely spaced; deep purple
SPORES White
SMELL Not distinctive

Wood Blewit

Lepista nuda (edible)

HABITAT Broadleaved and coniferous woodland, parkland
OCCURRENCE Autumn–winter; very common

CAP 6–12cm across; convex then flat, depressed or wavy;
  bluish-lilac, brownish later
STEM 5–9cm long x 15–25mm thick; slightly bulbous; bluish-
  lilac, covered with small fibres
FLESH Bluish-lilac
GILLS Narrowly attached and notched at stem;
  bluish-lilac fading to buff
SPORES Pale pink
SMELL Strong, perfumed

SIMILAR SPECIES

Bruising Webcap *Cortinarius purpurascens*
(inedible) is similar in size, has bluish-lilac
gills turning rusty brown (see page 37).
Cap joined to stem by white cobweb-like
threads when young.

Field Blewit

Lepista saeva (edible)

HABITAT Meadows and pasture, in groups or rings
OCCURRENCE Autumn–winter; occasional

CAP 5–10cm across; convex then flat, depressed or wavy; pallid
  to dirty brown
STEM 3–6cm long x 15–25mm; swollen at base; bluish-lilac,
  covered with small fibres
FLESH White to flesh-coloured
GILLS Narrowly attached and notched at
  stem; white to flesh-coloured
SPORES Pale pink
SMELL Strong, perfumed

SIMILAR SPECIES

Flowery Blewit *Lepista irina* (edible) is an
uncommon fungus similar in size, but has
a pallid stem with no lilac hues at all.
Found in open woodland and meadows in
groups or rings.

Pearly Parachute
Marasmius wynnei (inedible)

HABITAT Clustered in leaf litter, beech woodland
OCCURRENCE Autumn; occasional

CAP 2–6cm across; hemispherical to flattened-convex;
pale violet-grey drying milky white from centre,
edged with fine lines
STEM 2–10cm long x 2–5mm thick; reddish-brown,
buff at top
FLESH White in cap
GILLS Narrowly attached and notched at stem,
widely spaced; white then pale grey
SPORES White
SMELL Hay or cut grass

SIMILAR SPECIES

Redleg Toughshank *Collybia
erythropus* (inedible) has a
smaller cap (1–3cm across),
similar colour, drying wrinkled,
but without fine lines at edge.
Stem dark red, paler at top. Gills
free of stem. Grows in tufts in leaf
litter of broadleaved woodland.

Porcelain Fungus
Oudemansiella mucida (edible if washed)

HABITAT In clusters, usually high up, on beech trees
OCCURRENCE Late summer–autumn; common

CAP 2–8cm across; convex then flat; translucent and
very slimy; pale greyish-white becoming more
white, sometimes with an ochre tinge
STEM 3–10cm long x 3–10mm thick; very
tough; whitish with a small ring
FLESH White and thin
GILLS Broadly attached to stem, widely
spaced; white
SPORES White
SMELL Not distinctive

SIMILAR SPECIES

Some white or pale-coloured
bonnet *Mycena* species grow on
wood but are not slimy nor have
a ring on the stem (see page 21).

Saffrondrop Bonnet
Mycena crocata (inedible)

HABITAT In leaf litter in broadleaved woodland on chalk or limestone soils, mainly with beech
OCCURRENCE Autumn; occasional

CAP 1–3cm across; conical then bell-shaped; brownish-grey, staining orange
STEM 4–10cm long x 2–3mm thick; saffron orange, exuding an orange liquid when broken
FLESH Saffron orange, thin
GILLS Almost free of stem; white, staining orange
SPORES White
SMELL None

SIMILAR SPECIES

Bleeding Bonnet *Mycena sanguinolenta* (inedible), found amongst moss mainly in coniferous woodland, is of similar size. Stem exudes a blood-red liquid when broken.
Burgundydrop Bonnet *Mycena haematopus* (inedible), found on tree stumps, is slightly larger and has a brown-pink cap. Stem exudes a burgundy-red liquid when broken.

Yellowleg Bonnet
Mycena epipterygia (inedible)

HABITAT In grass or amongst moss in broadleaved and coniferous woodland, and heathland
OCCURRENCE Autumn; common

CAP 1–2cm across; convex to bell-shaped; fawn with fine lines and a delicately toothed, pale edge
STEM 4–7cm long x 1–2mm thick; very sticky; pale yellow
FLESH Very thin
GILLS Almost free of stem; pale pinkish
SPORES White
SMELL Not distinctive

SIMILAR SPECIES

There are many **bonnet** *Mycena* species of similar size found in grass or amongst moss, but the delicately toothed edge to the cap and the sticky, pale yellow stem make this species distinctive.

Common Bonnet
Mycena galericulata (inedible)

HABITAT In clusters, on fallen branches and stumps of broadleaved trees
OCCURRENCE All year; very common

CAP 2–6cm across; conical to bell-shaped with a broad central hump; pale brown to grey-brown, edged with fine lines
STEM 2–10cm long x 3–8mm thick; hollow and tough; pale brown to grey-brown
FLESH White and thin
GILLS Broadly attached to stem with a small tooth; white then flesh-pink
SPORES Cream
SMELL Mealy

SIMILAR SPECIES

Clustered Bonnet *Mycena inclinata* (inedible) grows in dense clusters on oak stumps. Cap similar colour but smaller (2–3cm across). Stem deep red-brown with a pale top. Smells rancid. *Mycena alcalina* (inedible), also found on stumps, is pale greyish-brown (see cover photo).

Rosy Bonnet
Mycena rosea (poisonous)

HABITAT In leaf litter in broadleaved woodland
OCCURRENCE Late summer–early winter; common

CAP 2–6cm across; convex then flatter with a broad central hump; rose pink drying paler, edged with fine lines
STEM 3–10cm long x 4–10mm thick; pale pink, base covered in white fibres
FLESH White
GILLS Broadly attached to stem; pink
SPORES White
SMELL Unpleasant

SIMILAR SPECIES

Lilac Bonnet *Mycena pura* (**poisonous**) is lilac to lilac-grey in colour and is similar in size and shape. Common in broadleaved and coniferous woodland, often with beech. *Mycena diosma* (**poisonous**), an uncommon species, found mainly in beech woodland, is a darker lilac-brown in colour.

Birch Knight
Tricholoma fulvum (inedible)

HABITAT Broadleaved and mixed woodland, mainly with birch
OCCURRENCE Autumn–early winter; very common

CAP 4–8cm across; convex with a slight central hump; slimy
when wet; brown to reddish-brown, streaky
STEM 3–7cm long x 8–14mm thick; fibrous; reddish-brown
FLESH Whitish in cap, lemon yellow in stem
GILLS Narrowly attached and notched at stem; lemon yellow,
spotted brownish later
SPORES White
SMELL Mealy

SIMILAR SPECIES

Burnt Knight *Tricholoma ustale*
(**poisonous**), found mainly in beech
woodland, is similar in size, has a chestnut-
brown cap (also slimy in wet weather) and
white gills becoming rust-spotted.

22

Soapy Knight
Tricholoma saponaceum (inedible)

HABITAT Broadleaved and coniferous woodland, sometimes
in troops
OCCURRENCE Late summer–autumn; occasional

CAP 5–10cm across; convex then flatter with a broad central
hump; grey-brown, often with an olive tint
STEM 3–10cm long x 10–30mm thick; whitish with reddish
or olive tint
FLESH White, later pinkish
GILLS Narrowly attached and
notched at stem; widely
spaced; whitish
SPORES White
SMELL Soapy

SIMILAR SPECIES

Deceiving Knight *Tricholoma sejunctum*
(inedible), occasionally found in
broadleaved woodland, usually with oak, is
similar in size, but does not smell of soap.
Cap is a streaky yellowish-green, darker
olive-brown in centre.

Sulphur Knight
Tricholoma sulphureum (**poisonous**)

HABITAT Broadleaved woodland, mainly with oak, occasionally in coniferous woodland
OCCURRENCE Autumn–early winter; common

CAP 3–8cm across; convex with a small central hump; sulphur yellow, often tinged red-brown
STEM 2.5–4cm long x 6–10mm thick; sulphur yellow with red-brown fibres
FLESH Yellow
GILLS Narrowly attached and notched at the stem, widely spaced; yellow
SPORES White
SMELL Strong, coalgas

SIMILAR SPECIES
The yellow colour of the Sulphur Knight combined with its strong coalgas smell makes it difficult to mistake for other woodland species.

Plums and Custard
Tricholomopsis rutilans (inedible)

HABITAT On and around rotting conifer stumps
OCCURRENCE Late summer–autumn; common

CAP 4–12cm across; convex often with a low, broad central hump; yellow, covered in reddish-purple scales
STEM 3–5.5cm long x 10–15mm thick; yellow covered in reddish-purple scales
FLESH Creamy-yellow
GILLS Narrowly attached to stem; custard yellow
SPORES White
SMELL Rotting wood

SIMILAR SPECIES
The reddish-purple and yellow colour combination together with the habitat preference of Plums and Custard make it unmistakable.

False Deathcap
Amanita citrina (inedible)

HABITAT Broadleaved and coniferous woodland, especially with beech

OCCURRENCE Summer–late autumn; common

CAP 4–10cm across; rounded then flat; ivory (sometimes white) to pale lemon, covered in whitish patches which discolour brownish

STEM 6–8cm long x 8–12mm thick; with a ring, bulbous base enclosed in a cup-like sack; whitish

FLESH White

GILLS Narrowly attached to stem, whitish

SPORES White

SMELL Strong, of raw potato

SIMILAR SPECIES

Deathcap *Amanita phalloides* (deadly poisonous) is similar in size, but cap is yellowish-green to olive (sometimes quite pale) with no patches, stem flushed with cap colour, smell sickly sweet (see below). **Destroying Angel** *Amanita virosa* (deadly poisonous) is similar but pure white.

Deathcap
Amanita phalloides (deadly poisonous)

HABITAT Broadleaved woodland, especially with oak

OCCURRENCE Late summer–autumn; occasional

CAP 4–12cm across; rounded then flat; yellowish-green to olive (sometimes much paler), often with a streaked appearance

STEM 3–13cm long x 10–18mm thick; with a ring, bulbous base enclosed in a cup-like sack; flushed cap colour

FLESH White

GILLS Free of stem; white

SPORES White

SMELL Sickly sweet

SIMILAR SPECIES

False Deathcap *Amanita citrina* (inedible) (see above). **Wood Mushroom** *Agaricus silvicola* (edible) is similar in size and shape (see page 31). Cap is cream, bruising ochre. Stem whitish with large ring, but no cup-like sack at base. Gills are free of stem, pale pink-grey, later dark brown. Smells of aniseed.

The Blusher
Amanita rubescens (**poisonous** if eaten raw – best avoided)

HABITAT Broadleaved and coniferous woodland
OCCURRENCE Summer–autumn; very common

CAP 5–15cm across; rounded then flat; reddish-brown
(sometimes paler), covered in whitish to pale
reddish-brown patches
STEM 6–14cm long x 10–25mm thick; with a ring,
bulbous base sometimes has scaly patches;
whitish, flushed reddish-brown
FLESH White, becoming pink when bruised
or broken
GILLS Free of stem; white, becoming spotted
reddish when bruised or broken
SPORES White
SMELL Not distinctive

SIMILAR SPECIES

Grey Spotted Amanita
Amanita excelsa (inedible) is
similar in size, has greyish-brown
cap covered in pale grey patches.
Panthercap *Amanita pantherina*
(**poisonous**) is smaller, with
brown cap covered in white warts.
Both species do not bruise pinkish.

Fly Agaric
Amanita muscaria (**poisonous**)

HABITAT Broadleaved woodland and scattered trees in
parkland or heathland, usually with birch
OCCURRENCE Late summer–autumn;
very common

CAP 8–20cm across; rounded then flat;
bright red, covered in white pointed
warts (often washed away by rain)
STEM 8–18cm long x 10–20mm thick;
with a ring, bulbous base
with scaly patches; whitish
FLESH White, tinged red below cap skin
GILLS Free of stem; white
SPORES White
SMELL Not distinctive

SIMILAR SPECIES

Orange grisette *Amanita
crocea* (edible), occasionally
found in broadleaved woodland
(usually with birch), is slightly
smaller, has yellow-orange cap
with no white warts, yellow-
orange stem and cream gills.
Many **brittlegill** *Russula* species
(see page 46) have a red cap,
white stem and white gills.

Snakeskin Grisette
Amanita ceciliae (**poisonous**)

HABITAT Open broadleaved woodland
OCCURRENCE Autumn; rare

CAP 7–12cm across; convex then bell-shaped;
greyish-brown with grooved edge,
covered in large, grey, felty patches
STEM 7.5–13cm long x 15–20mm thick;
bulbous base; grey-brown with white,
shaggy bands, giving a snakeskin appearance
(hence the name)
FLESH White
GILLS Free of stem; white
SPORES White
SMELL Not distinctive

SIMILAR SPECIES

Amanita submembranacea
(**poisonous**), occasionally found
in broadleaved and coniferous
woodland, is slightly smaller, has
a browner cap and paler stem.

Tawny Grisette
Amanita fulva (edible, but best avoided)

HABITAT Open broadleaved woodland, often
with birch, but also beech and oak
OCCURRENCE Autumn; common

CAP 4–9cm across; rounded then flat with
a low central hump, edge distinctly
grooved; orange-brown
STEM 7–12cm long x 8–12mm thick; tapering,
base enclosed in a large cup-like sack; white
flushed cap colour
FLESH White
GILLS Free of stem; white
SPORES White
SMELL Not distinctive

SIMILAR SPECIES

Grisette *Amanita vaginata*
(edible but best avoided),
occasionally found in broadleaved
woodland, is similar in size and
shape, but has grey-brown cap.
The rarer **Orange Grisette**
Amanita crocea (edible) has
yellow-orange cap and stem.

Indigo Pinkgill

Entoloma chalybaeum (**poisonous**)

HABITAT Grassland, heathland and open woodland, often amongst moss
OCCURRENCE Autumn; occasional

CAP 1–2.5cm across; convex; blue-black, darker in the centre, covered in darker radiating fibres, edged with fine lines
STEM 3–4cm long x 1–2mm thick; dark blue to blue-black
FLESH Dark blue, thin
GILLS Narrowly attached and notched at the stem; pale blue-grey to blue, pinkish-brown later
SPORES Pink
SMELL Mushroomy

SIMILAR SPECIES

Blue Edge Pinkgill *Entoloma serrulatum* (**poisonous**) lawns, meadows and grass verges, is similar in size, but the blue-black cap becomes browner and has a central depression, gills have a blackish edge.

Mousepee Pinkgill

Entoloma incanum (**poisonous**)

HABITAT Grassland and meadows on chalk or limestone
OCCURRENCE Late summer–autumn; occasional

CAP 1–3cm across; convex then flat, dimpled in the centre; yellow-brown to olive-brown, darker in centre, edged with fine lines
STEM 2–4cm long x 1–3mm thick; yellowish-green, bruising bluish-green
FLESH Greenish and thin
GILLS Broadly attached to stem; greenish-white, later flesh coloured
SPORES Pale pink
SMELL Strong, of mice

SIMILAR SPECIES

Parrot Waxcap *Hygrocybe psittacina* (inedible), also found in grassland and meadows, is similar in size (see page 9). Cap is slimy, green at first, then yellowish-green. Stem is green to blue-green. Gills white tinged yellow-green.

Skullcap Dapperling
Leucocoprinus brebissonii (inedible)

HABITAT Broadleaved woodland
OCCURRENCE Autumn; occasional

CAP 2–3cm across; conical then flattened; edge grooved; white and delicate, with a grey-brown central disc and small, grey-brown scales
STEM 4.5–6cm long x 3–6mm thick; with a small ring and thickened towards base; white
FLESH White
GILLS Free of stem; white
SPORES White
SMELL Not distinctive

SIMILAR SPECIES

Stinking Dapperling *Lepiota cristata* (**poisonous**), common in woodland, has a more bell-shaped, creamy-white cap with reddish-brown centre. Smell unpleasant. *Lepiota felina* (**poisonous**), found occasionally in coniferous woodland, has a creamy-white cap with blackish-brown scales and centre.

Lilac Dapperling
Cystolepiota bucknallii (**poisonous**)

HABITAT Damp broadleaved woodland and scrub on chalk or limestone
OCCURRENCE Autumn; uncommon

CAP 2–4cm across; conical to convex with a broad central hump; mealy; whitish tinged lilac-violet when young
STEM 2–4.5cm long x 3–5mm thick; mealy; lilac-violet, whitish at top
FLESH Whitish to lilac
GILLS Free of stem; cream
SPORES White
SMELL Strong, coalgas

SIMILAR SPECIES

Lilac Fibrecap *Inocybe geophylla* var. *lilacina* (**poisonous**), found along woodland paths (see page 40), is pale lilac and similar in size, but does not have the strong coalgas smell of the Lilac Dapperling.

Green Dapperling
Lepiota grangei (poisonous)

HABITAT Broadleaved woodland, often in coppiced areas
OCCURRENCE Late summer–autumn; rare

CAP 1–3.5cm across; conical then flattened; cream, with blackish-brown to greenish scales
STEM 2.5–6cm long x 3–5mm thick; swollen base; cream, staining orange, with greenish scales towards base
FLESH Whitish
GILLS Free of stem; cream
SPORES White
SMELL Unpleasant

Freckled Dapperling
Lepiota aspera (poisonous)

HABITAT Broadleaved woodland
OCCURRENCE Autumn; occasional

CAP 5–10cm across; rounded then bluntly conical to bell-shaped; dark brown in centre, breaking up into coarse, dark brown scales
STEM 3–5cm long x 5–10mm thick; with a white, cottony ring often sticking to the cap; brownish, covered in dark brown scales
FLESH White
GILLS Free of stem; crowded; white
SPORES White
SMELL Unpleasant

Shaggy Parasol

Macrolepiota rhacodes (edible, can cause stomach upsets)

HABITAT Mixed woodland, gardens, roadside verges
OCCURRENCE Late summer–autumn; common

CAP 5–15cm across; rounded then almost flat;
pale greyish-brown, shaggy with broad
scales on a fibrous background
STEM 10–15cm long x 10–15mm thick;
movable double ring, bulbous base;
whitish tinged pinkish-brown
FLESH White, turning orange-pink
GILLS Free of stem; white, bruising
reddish
SPORES White
SMELL Aromatic

SIMILAR SPECIES

Parasol *Macrolepiota procera*
(edible) is similar in size and
shape, but stem has a grey-
brown, felt-like, covering which
splits, giving it a snakeskin
appearance (see below).

30

Parasol

Macrolepiota procera (edible)

HABITAT Open woodland, meadows, pastures
OCCURRENCE Summer–autumn; common

CAP 10–25cm across; rounded then flat with prominent
central hump; buff to grey-brown, covered in darker,
shaggy scales
STEM 15–30cm long x 15–40mm thick; movable
double ring, bulbous base; whitish, covered
in grey-brown, felt-like covering which
splits, giving it a snakeskin appearance
FLESH White and thin
GILLS Free of stem; white
SPORES White
SMELL Not distinctive

SIMILAR SPECIES

Shaggy Parasol *Macrolepiota*
rhacodes (edible) is similar in
size and shape (see above).
Slender Parasol *Macrolepiota*
mastoidea (edible), found in
open woodland, is similar in
shape but smaller. Cap is white
to creamy-ochre.

Horse Mushroom
Agaricus arvensis (edible)

HABITAT Meadows, pastures, often in rings
OCCURRENCE Autumn; occasional

CAP 8–20cm across; rounded then convex to flat; creamy-white
STEM 8–10cm long x 3–10mm thick; with a ring, slightly club-shaped base; creamy-white
FLESH White and thick
GILLS Free of stem; whitish to pinkish-brown, later dark brown
SPORES Dark brown
SMELL Faintly aniseed

SIMILAR SPECIES

Field Mushroom *Agaricus campestris* (edible) is smaller (4–12cm across) with no aniseed smell; **Yellow Stainer** *Agaricus xanthodermus* (**poisonous**), whiter and edges of cap bruise bright yellow if scratched. Both are found in grassland.

Wood Mushroom
Agaricus silvicola (edible)

HABITAT Broadleaved and coniferous woodland
OCCURRENCE Autumn; occasional

CAP 5–10cm across; convex; cream, bruising ochre, becoming more yellow with age
STEM 5–8cm long x 10–15mm thick; with a large drooping ring, bulbous base; cream, bruising ochre
FLESH White and thin
GILLS Free of stem; greyish-pink, later dark brown
SPORES Dark brown
SMELL Aniseed

SIMILAR SPECIES

Yellow Stainer *Agaricus xanthodermus* (**poisonous**), whiter and edges of cap bruise bright yellow if scratched. **Deathcap** *Amanita phalloides* (**deadly poisonous**) has yellow-green to olive-green cap and stem, white gills (see page 24).

Shaggy Inkcap or Lawyer's Wig
Coprinus comatus (edible when young)

HABITAT Grassy areas, lawns, roadside verges
OCCURRENCE Late summer–autumn; very common

CAP 5–15cm high; cylindrical; white with buff centre, breaking into large shaggy scales
STEM 10–30cm long x 10–25mm thick; with a small ring; whitish
FLESH White
GILLS Free of stem; white then pinkish, finally black and inky
SPORES Brownish-black
SMELL Faint and pleasant

SIMILAR SPECIES

Snowy Inkcap *Coprinus niveus* (inedible), found in pastures on cow or horse dung, is much smaller. Cap is 1.5–3cm high, bell-shaped, with a white, chalky surface.

Common Inkcap
Coprinus atramentarius (poisonous)

HABITAT Woodland, parks and gardens, growing in tufts, often on buried wood
OCCURRENCE Spring–autumn; common

CAP 3–7cm high; oval to conical with puckered edge; streaky greyish, brownish in centre
STEM 7–17cm long x 9–13mm thick; whitish with dark ring-like marking near base
FLESH White
GILLS Free of stem, crowded; white then black and inky
SPORES Date brown
SMELL Faint and pleasant

SIMILAR SPECIES

Glistening Inkcap *Coprinus micaceus* (inedible) grows in clusters on stumps and buried wood of broadleaved trees. Smaller, cap is 1–4cm high, oval to bell-shaped, ochre to cinnamon in colour, centre covered in a white, glistening dusting when young.

Magpie Inkcap
Coprinus picaceus (edible)

HABITAT In leaf litter, mainly beech woodland on chalk or limestone

OCCURRENCE Late summer–autumn; occasional

CAP 5–8cm high; oval to conical bell-shaped; white on a dark grey-brown background, splitting into large patches, giving a chequered appearance

STEM 9–30cm long x 6–15mm thick; bulbous base; white

FLESH White

GILLS Free of stem, crowded; white then pinkish, finally black and inky

SPORES Black

SMELL Unpleasant

SIMILAR SPECIES

Hare's-foot Inkcap *Coprinus lagopus* (inedible), found in woodland, amongst leaf litter, is smaller. Cap is 2–4cm high, cylindrical to conical then almost flat, covered in white tufted fibres, breaking apart to show grey surface.

Fairy Inkcap
Coprinus disseminatus (inedible)

HABITAT Often in hundreds in dense clusters on, or nearby, stumps of broadleaved trees

OCCURRENCE Late spring–autumn; common

CAP 0.5–1.5cm high; oval to bell-shaped; buff to pale grey with reddish-brown centre, grooved edge

STEM 1.5–4cm long x 1–3mm thick; whitish with a downy base

FLESH Whitish and thin

GILLS Free of stem; white then grey-brown, finally black (but not inky)

SPORES Date brown

SMELL None

SIMILAR SPECIES

Common Stump Brittlestem *Psathyrella piluliformis* (inedible), common from late spring to autumn, grows in dense tufts on or near stumps of broadleaved tree. Cap is larger (2–3cm across), convex to flat, tan to chestnut and drying paler. Gills clay-brown to chocolate brown (not inky).

Sulphur Tuft
Hypholoma fasciculare (poisonous)

HABITAT In dense clusters, on stumps of broadleaved and coniferous trees
OCCURRENCE All year; very common

CAP 2–7cm across; convex; yellow, more orange-tan in centre
STEM 4–10cm long x 5–10mm thick; often curved; yellow at top, brownish at base
FLESH Sulphur yellow
GILLS Broadly attached to stem; sulphur yellow, later olive then dark brown
SPORES Purple-brown
SMELL Mushroomy

SIMILAR SPECIES

Conifer Tuft *Hypholoma capnoides* (inedible) grows on stumps of coniferous trees. Cap pale ochre, gills whitish then greyish-lilac.
Brick Tuft *Hypholoma lateritium* (inedible) grows on stumps of broadleaved trees. Cap ochre grading to brick-red in centre, gills yellowish then olive-brown. **Sheathed Woodtuft** *Kuehneromyces mutabilis* (edible) grows in dense clusters on stumps or trunks of broadleaved trees. Cap orange-brown drying from centre. Gills tan then cinnamon.

34

Shaggy Scalycap
Pholiota squarrosa (inedible)

HABITAT In dense clusters at base of broadleaved trees
OCCURRENCE Autumn; common

CAP 3–11cm across; convex then flat, edge rolls under; pale straw yellow, covered in rough, red-brown scales
STEM 5–12cm long x 10–15mm thick; narrowing to base; pale yellow with red-brown scales
FLESH Pale yellow, red-brown in base
GILLS Broadly attached to stem; pale yellow, cinnamon later
SPORES Rusty brown
SMELL Radish

SIMILAR SPECIES

Pholiota adiposa (inedible) grows in dense clusters on stumps and at base of beech trees. Cap is sticky, golden yellow and covered in rusty brown, gelatinous scales. **Alder Scalycap** *Pholiota alnicola* (inedible) grows in small tufts on broadleaved trees, especially alder, willow and birch. Cap is smaller (2–8cm across), bright lemon yellow, smooth and greasy.

Liberty Cap or Magic Mushroom
Psilocybe semilanceata (**poisonous**, hallucinogenic)

HABITAT Grassland, pastures, lawns, roadside verges
OCCURRENCE Late summer–autumn; common

CAP 0.5–1.5cm across; conical with a distinct
   sharp point in centre; yellowish-brown
   drying buff
STEM 2.5–7.5cm long x 1–2mm thick; cream
FLESH Cream to pale clay-brown
GILLS Broadly attached to stem; clay brown,
   dark purple-brown later
SPORES Dark purplish-brown
SMELL Not distinctive

SIMILAR SPECIES

There are many small brown
conical-capped fungi found in
grassland, particularly **conecap**
Conocybe species (inedible),
mottlegill *Panaeolus* species
(inedible) and several **bonnet**
Mycena species (inedible), but
the small, sharp point in the
centre of the cap, is a key feature
of Liberty Cap.

Verdigris Agaric
Stropharia aeruginosa (**poisonous**)

HABITAT Broadleaved and coniferous woodland, heathland, pastures
OCCURRENCE Late summer–autumn; occasional

CAP 2–8cm across; convex to bell-shaped then flat with a slight
   central hump; blue to blue-green, flecked with white
   scales, becoming yellowish once these are lost
STEM 4–10cm long x 4–12mm thick; with a small
   shaggy ring, smooth above and covered in white
   fibres below ring; whitish to blue
FLESH Whitish-blue
GILLS Broadly attached to stem; whitish
   then brown with a white edge
SPORES Purplish-brown
SMELL None

SIMILAR SPECIES

Blue Roundhead *Stropharia*
caerulea (inedible), found in
grassland and leaf litter, often
amongst nettles, has a sticky,
bluish-green to yellow-green cap,
soon changing to straw yellow.
Aniseed Funnel *Clitocybe odora*
(edible), found in broadleaved
and coniferous woodland, usually
in troops or rings, smells strongly
of aniseed (see page 13).

Purple Stocking Webcap
Cortinarius stillatitius (inedible)

HABITAT Broadleaved woodland, usually with beech
OCCURRENCE Autumn; occasional

CAP 3–8cm across; conical-convex, often with a central hump; slimy when wet, drying shiny; ochre to rich brown, edge often grooved
STEM 8–10cm long x 10–20mm thick; white, covered in a stocking-like, lilac-violet slimy skin, part-way up the stem
FLESH Whitish, tinged yellowish
GILLS Broadly attached to stem, to free of stem; clay brown then rusty brown
SPORES Rusty brown
SMELL None

SIMILAR SPECIES

The lilac-violet, stocking-like, slimy skin is a key feature of this species, although there are several other slimy-capped **webcap** *Cortinarius* species found in woodland (see below).

Yellow Webcap
Cortinarius delibutus (inedible)

HABITAT Broadleaved woodland, usually with beech or birch
OCCURRENCE Autumn; occasional

CAP 3–9cm across; convex then flatter, sometimes with a slight central hump; buff to yellow, slimy
STEM 3–10cm long x 7–15mm thick; whitish tinged yellow by the slimy veil, rusty ring marking from remains of the cobweb-like threads attached to the cap when young
FLESH White in stem, yellow in cap
GILLS Broadly attached to stem to free of stem; pale violet then soon yellowish-clay brown or cinnamon
SPORES Rusty brown
SMELL Faintly of radish

SIMILAR SPECIES

Birch Webcap *Cortinarius triumphans* (inedible), found in damp, broadleaved woodland, usually with birch, also yellow, is larger and more robust (see page 37).

Bruising Webcap
Cortinarius purpurascens (inedible)

HABITAT Broadleaved and coniferous woodland
OCCURRENCE Autumn; occasional

CAP 5–15cm across; rounded then flatter, with a broad central hump; buff-brown to brown, violet tinged and streaky; cobweb-like threads attached to stem when young
STEM 3–12cm long x 15–25mm thick; violet tinged with shaggy rusty brown ring marking, bulbous base
FLESH Pale violet-grey, bruising purple
GILLS Broadly attached to stem, to free of stem; lilac-violet, then clay-brown to cinnamon brown, bruising purple
SPORES Rusty brown
SMELL Not distinctive

SIMILAR SPECIES

Wood Blewit *Lepista nuda* (edible), found in broadleaved and coniferous woodland (see page 18), is similar in size, has bluish-lilac gills (not turning rusty brown). Cap is bluish-lilac, browner later. Smells strongly perfumed.

37

Birch Webcap
Cortinarius triumphans (inedible)

HABITAT Damp, broadleaved woodland, usually with birch
OCCURRENCE Autumn; occasional

CAP 5–12cm across; convex; pale yellow to golden yellow in centre; cobweb-like threads attached to stem when young
STEM 7–17cm long x 10–25mm thick; whitish above ring marking, yellowish with bands of reddish scales below
FLESH Creamy-yellow
GILLS Broadly attached to stem; cream, later rusty-buff
SPORES Rusty brown
SMELL Not distinctive

SIMILAR SPECIES

Spectacular Rustgill *Gymnopilus junonius* (inedible), found in dense clusters at base of broadleaved trees, is much larger (see page 39). Cap and stem golden-brown, gills yellow then rusty brown.

Pearly Webcap
Cortinarius alboviolaceus (inedible)

HABITAT Broadleaved woodland, often with birch
OCCURRENCE Autumn; occasional

CAP 3–9cm across; convex to bell-shaped with central hump; bluish-white to pale violet-grey, at first covered in whitish silky veil; cobweb-like threads attached to stem when young
STEM 8–10cm long x 10–18mm thick; swollen base; bluish-white to pale violet-grey, more violet near top
FLESH Pale violet-grey
GILLS Narrowly attached to stem; pale violet-grey then clay brown, later rusty brown
SPORES Rusty brown
SMELL Pleasant

SIMILAR SPECIES

Frosty Funnel *Clitocybe phyllophila* (**poisonous**), common, growing in troops or rings in broadleaved and coniferous woodland, is similar in size. Looks similar when young as cap is convex and covered in a white bloom, but soon becomes funnel-shaped. Whitish gills run down onto stem.

Bloodred Webcap
Cortinarius sanguineus (inedible)

HABITAT Broadleaved and coniferous woodland
OCCURRENCE Autumn; occasional

CAP 2–5cm across; convex; blood-red, covered in silky fibres; cobweb-like threads attached to stem when young
STEM 3–6cm long x 3–8mm thick; crimson to blood-red
FLESH Crimson to blood-red
GILLS Broadly attached to stem; blood-red, later rusty brown
SPORES Rusty brown
SMELL Faint, but pleasant

SIMILAR SPECIES

There are several red-brown to dark brown **webcap** *Cortinarius* species of similar size found in woodland, but the colour of the Bloodred Webcap makes it difficult to mistake for other webcaps.

Poisonpie
Hebeloma crustuliniforme (poisonous)

HABITAT Open mixed woodland, along woodland paths, parks, gardens
OCCURRENCE Late summer–autumn; very common

CAP 4–10cm across; convex then flatter, often with a central hump; greasy or slimy when wet; buff to tan, darker in centre
STEM 4–7cm long x 10–20mm thick; whitish with mealy flecks towards the top
FLESH White and thick
GILLS Broadly attached to narrowly attached to stem; clay brown, with watery droplets in damp conditions
SPORES Rusty brown
SMELL Radish

SIMILAR SPECIES

There are a number of similar *Hebeloma* species, including **Sweet Poisonpie** *Hebeloma pallidoluctosum* which has a sweet flowery smell, most however, can only be identified by microscopic features. **Field Mushroom** *Agaricus campestris* (edible) is similar in size. Stem has a ring, gills are pinkish-grey becoming dark brown.

Spectacular Rustgill
Gymnopilus junonius (inedible)

HABITAT In clusters on stumps and logs and at the base of broadleaved trees
OCCURRENCE Late summer–early winter; common

CAP 3–13cm across; convex then flatter; covered in small, fibrous scales; golden brown
STEM 3–12cm long x 15–30mm thick; fibrous, swollen in centre, with yellowish ring; yellow to ochre
FLESH Pale yellowish
GILLS Broadly attached to stem; yellow, later rusty
SPORES Rusty brown
SMELL Not distinctive

SIMILAR SPECIES

Common Rustgill *Gymnopilus penetrans* (inedible), found in coniferous woodland on stumps (not clustered) and debris, is similar in colour, but is much smaller (cap 3–8cm across).

White Fibrecap
Inocybe geophylla (poisonous)

HABITAT Open areas and paths in broadleaved and coniferous woodland
OCCURRENCE Late summer–autumn; very common

CAP 1.5–3.5cm across; conical then flatter with a central hump; smooth and silky; white, flushed yellowish at centre
STEM 1–6cm long x 3–6mm thick; white with silky fibres
FLESH White
GILLS Narrowly attached to stem, crowded; clay-brown
SPORES Brown
SMELL Earthy

SIMILAR SPECIES
Lilac Fibrecap *Inocybe geophylla* var. *lilacina*, found in same habitat, is the lilac form of this species (see below).

Lilac Fibrecap
Inocybe geophylla var. *lilacina* (poisonous)

HABITAT Open areas and paths in broadleaved and coniferous woodland
OCCURRENCE Late summer–autumn; very common

CAP 1.5–3.5cm across; conical then flatter with a central hump; smooth and silky; lilac, flushed ochre at centre
STEM 1–6cm long x 3–6mm thick; lilac with silky fibres
FLESH Lilac-grey
GILLS Narrowly attached to stem, crowded; clay-brown
SPORES Brown
SMELL Earthy

SIMILAR SPECIES
Amethyst Deceiver *Laccaria amethystina* (edible), found in broadleaved and coniferous woodland, is deep purple, fading to more lilac-buff when dry, gills are deep purple (see page 17).

Star Fibrecap
Inocybe asterospora (**poisonous**)

HABITAT Broadleaved woodland, especially oak
OCCURRENCE Late summer–autumn; occasional

CAP 4–6cm across; conical then flatter, with a central hump; often splitting at edge, radially streaked, centre almost smooth; reddish-brown to chestnut
STEM 4–7cm long x 4–7mm thick; with a rimmed, basal bulb; reddish-brown with a mealy surface
FLESH White and thick
GILLS Narrowly attached to stem; clay-brown, later darker brown
SPORES Star-shaped, brown
SMELL Mealy

SIMILAR SPECIES

Bulbous Fibrecap *Inocybe napipes* (**poisonous**), found in damp broadleaved and mixed woodland, is similar in shape and colour. Stem is whitish at top, flushed pale brown below and also has a rimmed, basal bulb. Under the microscope the spores are oblong and knobbly (not star-shaped).

41

Woolly Fibrecap
Inocybe lanuginosa (**poisonous**)

HABITAT Mixed woodland with pine and birch
OCCURRENCE Autumn; occasional

CAP 2–4cm across; convex, later flattened; covered in shaggy, fibrous, eract scales, especially in the centre; cinnamon to darker brown
STEM 4–7cm long x 3–7mm thick; brown, covered in cottony fibres, giving a coarse, shaggy appearance
FLESH White
GILLS Narrowly attached to broadly attached to stem; whitish, then cinnamon
SPORES Brown
SMELL Faint

SIMILAR SPECIES

Scaly Fibrecap *Inocybe hystrix* (**poisonous**), found in broadleaved woodland, especially with beech, is similar in size and appearance. **Torn Fibrecap** *Inocybe lacera* (**poisonous**), found on sandy soils, especially with pine, has a walnut-brown cap covered in fibres.

Woolly Milkcap
Lactarius torminosus (poisonous)

HABITAT Woodland and heathland, usually with birch
OCCURRENCE Late summer–autumn; common

CAP 4–12cm across; convex then funnel-shaped; edge rolled
under and covered in woolly fibres; salmon-buff to pink with
deeper-coloured concentric bands; exudes a milky liquid
when broken
STEM 4–8cm long x 10–20mm thick; becoming hollow; pale
flesh colour to salmon
FLESH White; milk hot and bitter, white
GILLS Running slightly down onto stem; pale pink-buff
SPORES Pale ochre, tinged salmon
SMELL Faint, like turpentine

SIMILAR SPECIES

Bearded Milkcap *Lactarius pubescens*
(**poisonous**) grows near birch trees on
sandy soils. Similar size and shape but cap
is creamy-white to pinkish-buff, hairy not
woolly. Milk is white and very hot.

Grey Milkcap
Lactarius vietus (inedible)

HABITAT With birch trees in damp places
OCCURRENCE Autumn; common

CAP 2.5–7cm across; flattened-convex then funnel-shaped;
slimy when wet; violet-grey to pinkish-grey with brownish
tints; exudes a milky liquid when broken
STEM 2.5–8cm long x 5–13mm thick; weak and often hollow;
whitish, tinged pinkish-grey
FLESH Whitish-buff; milk hot and
bitter, white drying greyish
GILLS Running slightly down onto
stem; whitish to buff
SPORES Creamy-white,
tinged salmon
SMELL Not distinctive

SIMILAR SPECIES

Fiery Milkcap *Lactarius pyrogalus*
(inedible), only found with hazel, has a
smoky-grey to pinkish-buff cap, with
indistinct concentric bands. Gills are pale
apricot and run down onto stem. Milk is
fiery hot (hence the name).

Oakbug Milkcap
Lactarius quietus (inedible)

HABITAT With oak trees
OCCURRENCE Late summer–autumn; very common

CAP 3–8cm across; convex then flat with shallow depression; dry and matt; dull reddish-brown with darker concentric bands; exudes a milky liquid when broken
STEM 4–9cm long x 10–15mm thick; often hollow; dull reddish-brown
FLESH Whitish-buff; milk mild, white
GILLS Running slightly down onto stem; brownish-white then reddish-brown
SPORES Cream
SMELL Faintly oily

SIMILAR SPECIES

Yellowdrop Milkcap *Lactarius chrysorrheus* (**poisonous**), also found with oak trees, is similar in colour, but white milk turns lemon yellow after a few minutes (hence the name) and is slowly bitter and hot (see page 45).

Ugly Milkcap
Lactarius turpis (inedible)

HABITAT Usually with birch trees in damp places
OCCURRENCE Late summer–autumn; very common

CAP 5–20cm across; flattened-convex, later with a shallow depression; sticky and slimy; dark olive-brown to olive-blackish; exudes a milky liquid when broken
STEM 4–8cm long x 10–25mm thick; short and stout; dark olive-brown to olive-blackish
FLESH White; milk very hot and bitter, white and abundant
GILLS Running down onto stem; cream to yellowish-buff
SPORES Cream, tinged salmon
SMELL Not distinctive

SIMILAR SPECIES

The dirty, olive-brown colour, the abundant, hot and bitter milk, together with its association with birch trees, make the Ugly Milkcap difficult to mistake for other species.

Beech Milkcap
Lactarius blennius (inedible)

HABITAT Beech woodland and with beech in mixed woodland
OCCURRENCE Late summer–autumn; very common

CAP 4–10cm across; convex then flatter with a central
   depression; very slimy when wet; greenish-grey to pale
   greying-brown, often with darker blotches in concentric
   bands; exudes a milky liquid when broken
STEM 4–5cm long x 10–17mm thick; slimy; pale grey to whitish
FLESH Whitish; milk very hot and bitter, white
GILLS Running slightly down onto stem;
   whitish, later pale buff and bruising
   brownish-grey
SPORES Cream, tinged flesh
SMELL Not distinctive

SIMILAR SPECIES

Abundant Milkcap *Lactarius fluens*
(inedible) is occasionally found mainly
with beech. Cap is similar colour but with a
paler edge, sticky when wet, not slimy. Gills
narrowly attached to stem to running
slightly down onto stem, crowded, cream
then creamy-buff, bruising brown after
several hours.

44

Orange Milkcap
Lactarius aurantiacus (inedible)

HABITAT Broadleaved and coniferous woodland
OCCURRENCE Late summer–autumn; common

CAP 3–6cm across; convex then flat with a slight depression,
   sometimes with a small central hump; greasy; bright orange
   to brownish-orange; exudes a milky liquid when broken
STEM 3–7cm long x 6–12mm thick; orange to brownish-orange
FLESH White; milk mild, white and abundant
GILLS Broadly attached to stem to running slightly
   down onto stem; pale ochre
SPORES Cream, tinged salmon
SMELL Not distinctive

SIMILAR SPECIES

False Saffron Milkcap *Lactarius
deterrimus* (edible), found in coniferous
woodland with spruce, is larger. Cap is
convex later depressed, buff-orange,
bruising green. Gills run slightly onto stem
and are orange, bruising green. Milk is
carrot coloured and mild then bitter.

Watery Milkcap
Lactarius serifluus (inedible)

HABITAT With oak and beech trees
OCCURRENCE Late summer–autumn; occasional

CAP 3–7cm across; flattened-convex then slightly funnel-shaped; dry, matt and slightly wrinkled to lumpy; dull dark brown; exudes a cloudy liquid when broken
STEM 2–6.5cm long x 7–12mm thick; hollow; brown
FLESH Cinnamon-buff; milk mild, watery and cloudy
GILLS Running down onto stem; saffron to orange-cinnamon
SPORES Cream, tinged salmon
SMELL Oily

SIMILAR SPECIES

Liver Milkcap *Lactarius hepaticus* (inedible), found with pine and sometimes with spruce, is similar in size. Cap is dry and matt, liver coloured to dull chestnut brown. Milk is bitter and slightly hot, white and drying yellowish.

Yellowdrop Milkcap
Lactarius chrysorrheus (**poisonous**)

HABITAT With oak trees
OCCURRENCE Summer–autumn; common

CAP 3–8cm across; convex with a depression; pale salmon-rose to ochre-buff, with darker blotches and concentric bands; exudes a milky liquid when broken
STEM 3–8cm long x 9–20mm thick; hollow; whitish to pale buff
FLESH Whitish; milk slowly bitter and hot, white becoming sulphur yellow after 15 seconds
GILLS Running down onto stem, crowded; pinkish-buff
SPORES Creamy, tinged salmon
SMELL Not distinctive

SIMILAR SPECIES

Oakbug Milkcap *Lactarius quietus* (inedible), found with oak trees, is similar in size (see page 43). Cap is pinkish-brown with darker concentric bands. Milk is mild, white and does not change colour.

Beechwood Sickener
Russula nobilis (**poisonous**)

HABITAT Beech woodland and with beech in mixed woodland
OCCURRENCE Autumn; common

CAP 3–9cm across; convex then flat with shallow depression; sticky when wet, skin peels one-third in from edge; red to pink, sometimes almost white (especially after rain)
STEM 2.5–4.5cm long x 10–15mm thick; hard; white
FLESH White, pink under cap skin; taste hot
GILLS Narrowly attached to stem; brittle; white, later cream
SPORES Whitish
SMELL Coconut when young

SIMILAR SPECIES

The Sickener *Russula emetica* (**poisonous**), found with pines, has a cherry red cap. **Bloody Brittlegill** *Russula sanguinaria* (inedible), found with conifers, has a white stem often flushed pink or red. **Bleached Brittlegill** *Russula exalbicans* (inedible), found with birch trees, has a rose red to dull wine red cap fading to greenish-white or buff.

46

Purple Brittlegill
Russula atropurpurea (edible if cooked)

HABITAT Broadleaved and coniferous woodland
OCCURRENCE Summer–autumn; very common

CAP 4–10cm across; convex then flat with a shallow depression; sticky when wet; deep purplish-red with almost black centre
STEM 3–6cm long x 10–20mm thick; firm; softer later; white becoming grey with age
FLESH White; taste mild to moderately hot
GILLS Narrowly attached to stem; brittle; pale cream
SPORES Whitish
SMELL Faintly fruity

SIMILAR SPECIES

Other purplish-capped brittlegill *Russula* species include **Fragile Brittlegill** *Russula fragilis* (inedible), found with broadleaved and coniferous trees, smaller with a purple-violet tinted cap, and **Primrose Brittlegill** *Russula sardonia* (inedible), found with pine, has pale lilac stem and primrose yellow gills.

Fruity Brittlegill
Russula queletii (inedible)

HABITAT With spruce and pine trees
OCCURRENCE Summer–autumn; occasional

CAP 4–10cm across; convex then flat with shallow depression; skin peels halfway to two-thirds in from edge; purplish-red to brownish-red, paling after rain
STEM 3–8cm long x 10–15mm thick; slightly club-shaped; purplish-red to brownish-red
FLESH White; taste very hot
GILLS Broadly attached to stem; brittle; pale cream
SPORES Cream
SMELL Stewed fruit

SIMILAR SPECIES

Primrose Brittlegill *Russula sardonia* (inedible), found with pine, has pale lilac stem and primrose yellow gills. Smells slightly fruity.

Green Brittlegill
Russula aeruginea (edible)

HABITAT With birch trees, often in damp woodland
OCCURRENCE Summer–autumn; common

CAP 4–9cm across; convex then flat with a depression; skin peels to halfway in from edge; grass green, sometimes with brownish tinges, centre darker
STEM 4–8cm long x 7–20mm thick; firm; white
FLESH White; taste mild to slightly hot
GILLS Almost free of stem; brittle; whitish to cream
SPORES Cream
SMELL Not distinctive

SIMILAR SPECIES

Greencracked Brittlegill *Russula virescens* (edible), found in broadleaved woodland, usually with beech, has a rounded to flattish cap, grey-green to dull green, surface cracking into angular scales.

Charcoal Burner
Russula cyanoxantha (edible)

HABITAT Broadleaved woodland
OCCURRENCE Summer–autumn; very common

CAP 5–15cm across; rounded then flatter with a depression; skin peels halfway in from edge; very variable in colour, usually a mixture of dull lilac, purplish, wine-coloured, olive and brownish
STEM 5–10cm long x 15–30mm thick; hard; white
FLESH White; taste mild
GILLS Narrowly attached to stem; flexible; white to pale cream
SPORES Whitish
SMELL Not distinctive

SIMILAR SPECIES

Oilslick Brittlegill *Russula ionochlora* (edible), found with beech trees, has a cap typically zoned with a mixture of dull bluish, lilac and greenish-yellow. Flesh is white, taste hot when young. **Powdery Brittlegill** *Russula parazurea* (edible), found with broadleaved trees, has a bluish-grey to greenish-grey cap, matt and often powdery, peeling to two-thirds in from edge.

48

Ochre Brittlegill
Russula ochroleuca (edible)

HABITAT Broadleaved and coniferous woodland
OCCURRENCE Late summer–autumn; very common

CAP 4–10cm across; convex then flatter with a depression; skin peels to two-thirds in from edge; yellow ochre, sometimes greenish-yellow
STEM 4–7cm long x 15–25mm thick; white, greying with age
FLESH White; taste mild to moderately hot
GILLS Narrowly attached to stem; brittle; pale cream
SPORES Whitish to pale cream
SMELL Not distinctive

SIMILAR SPECIES

Yellow Swamp Brittlegill *Russula claroflava* (edible), found in damp birch woods, has a yellow, slightly shiny, cap. **Geranium Brittlegill** *Russula fellea* (inedible), found in beech woodland, has an ochre cap, stem and gills, smells of geranium leaves (see page 49).

Geranium Brittlegill
Russula fellea (inedible)

HABITAT Beech woodland
OCCURRENCE Late summer–autumn; common

CAP 4–9cm across; convex then flatter, often with a broad, low, central hump; slightly sticky when wet, skin peels only slightly in from edge; straw, buff to honey coloured
STEM 2–6cm long x 10–20mm thick; firm; pale cap-coloured
FLESH White; taste very hot
GILLS Narrowly attached to stem; brittle; pale cap-coloured
SPORES Whitish to pale cream
SMELL Geranium (Pelargonium) leaves

SIMILAR SPECIES

Ochre Brittlegill *Russula ochroleuca* (edible), found in broadleaved and coniferous woodland, has yellow ochre cap, white stem, pale cream gills and no distinctive smell (see page 44). **Stinking Brittlegill** *Russula foetens*, found in broadleaved and coniferous woodland. Cap is larger (5–12cm across), slimy and honey coloured. Smell oily, rancid.

Blackening Brittlegill
Russula nigricans (edible when young)

HABITAT Broadleaved and coniferous woodland
OCCURRENCE Summer–autumn; common

CAP 5–20cm across; convex then with a depression; off-white, then brownish and finally black
STEM 3–8cm long x 10–40mm thick; hard; off-white, then brownish and finally black
FLESH White, greyish-coral when broken, finally black
GILLS Broadly attached to stem; brittle, very thick and widely spaced; off-white, then brownish and finally black
SPORES Creamy white
SMELL Slightly fishy

SIMILAR SPECIES

Anthracite Brittlegill *Russula anthracina* (edible), occasionally found in broadleaved and coniferous woodland, also blackens with age, but is smaller and the gills are narrow and closely spaced.

Cep or Penny Bun
Boletus edulis (edible)

HABITAT Broadleaved and coniferous woodland
OCCURRENCE Summer–autumn; common

CAP 8–25cm across; bun-shaped to convex; smooth and dry, greasy when wet; brown
STEM 3–23cm long x 30–80mm thick; swollen at base; cream to pale brown, covered in a white netting
FLESH White
PORES Small and round; white, turning greenish-yellow with age
SPORES Olive brown
SMELL Pleasant

SIMILAR SPECIES

The rare **Dark Cep** *Boletus aereus* (edible), found with broadleaved trees, especially beech and oak, is similar in size and shape, but has a bay brown to dark brown cap, and a reddish-brown stem covered in a brown netting. **Bay Bolete** *Boletus badius* has lemon pores that bruise blue-green (see below).

Bay Bolete
Boletus badius (edible)

HABITAT Broadleaved and coniferous woodland
OCCURRENCE Late summer–autumn; very common

CAP 4–14cm across; bun-shaped to convex; smooth, slightly sticky when wet; bay brown to reddish-brown
STEM 4.5–12cm long x 8–40mm thick; bay brown or slightly paler
FLESH White, lemon yellow when cut, later faintly blue
PORES Large; cream to lemon yellow, bruising blue-green
SPORES Olive brown
SMELL Mushroomy

SIMILAR SPECIES

The rare **Dark Cep** *Boletus aereus* (edible), found with broadleaved trees, especially beech and oak, is similar in size, has a bay brown to dark brown cap, and a thick, reddish-brown stem covered in a brown netting, and swollen at the base.

Inkstain Bolete

Boletus pulverulentus (edible)

HABITAT Open broadleaved woodland, especially with oak
OCCURRENCE Late summer–autumn; occasional

CAP 4–9cm across; bun-shaped to convex; downy then
smooth; dull coffee to walnut brown, rapidly
bruising dark blue to almost black
STEM 5–6.5cm long x 8–14mm thick; yellow at
top, brownish elsewhere, streaked red-brown,
rapidly bruising dark blue then black
FLESH Lemon yellow, turning blue
when cut
PORES Bright lemon yellow, bruising
dark blue
SPORES Olive brown
SMELL Pleasant

SIMILAR SPECIES

Other bolete species found in
broadleaved woodland that
rapidly bruise blue-black include
Scarletina Bolete *Boletus
luridiformis* (inedible) with red
pores (see page 52) and **Lurid
Bolete** *Boletus luridus* (inedible)
with orange pores.

51

Bitter Beech Bolete

Boletus calopus (inedible)

HABITAT Broadleaved woodland, mainly with beech
OCCURRENCE Late summer–autumn; occasional

CAP 5–15cm across; bun-shaped to convex;
smoky grey-buff, smooth, sometimes scaly or
cracked later
STEM 7–10cm long x 35–45mm thick;
crimson, lemon yellow at top
FLESH Straw to pale lemon, white
then flushed blue when cut
PORES Sulphur yellow, bruising
bluish-green
SPORES Olive brown
SMELL Not distinctive

SIMILAR SPECIES

The rare **Devil's Bolete** *Boletus
satanus* (poisonous, possibly
deadly), is found with
broadleaved trees, especially
beech and oak. Cap (8–25cm
across) whitish flushed buff,
bruising brown. Stem red, orange
at top. Pores blood-red, orange
near edge, bruising greenish.
Flesh is straw, sky blue when cut.

Scarletina Bolete
Boletus luridiformis (inedible)

HABITAT Broadleaved and coniferous woodland
OCCURRENCE Late summer–autumn; common

CAP 8–20cm across; bun-shaped then flatter; slightly velvety then smooth, slightly sticky when wet; bay brown to walnut brown, bruising blue-black
STEM 4.5–14cm long x 20–50mm thick; yellowish, densely covered in red dots
FLESH Yellow, turning dark blue when cut
PORES Small, round; orange-red to rusty, bruising blue-black
SPORES Olive brown
SMELL Not distinctive

SIMILAR SPECIES

Lurid Bolete *Boletus luridus* (inedible), is similar in size and is found in broadleaved woodland and grassland on chalk or limestone, mainly with oak or beech. It also bruises blue-black and has orange pores and a downy, brown cap that becomes shiny. The lemon yellow flesh turns dark blue to greenish-blue when cut.

52

Red Cracking Bolete
Boletus chrysenteron (edible)

HABITAT Broadleaved and coniferous woodland
OCCURRENCE Late summer–autumn; common

CAP 4–11cm across; bun-shaped then flatter; slightly velvety then smooth; brown to buff, cracking to show coral pink flesh (hence the name)
STEM 4–8cm long x 10–15mm thick; red, lemon yellow at top
FLESH lemon yellow in cap turning slightly bluish, coral pink just below cap
PORES Large and angular; lemon yellow, bruising greenish
SPORES Olive brown
SMELL Not distinctive

SIMILAR SPECIES

Ruby Bolete *Boletus rubellus* (edible), occasionally found in damp areas in broadleaved woodland, usually with oak, has a small (2–6cm across), blood-red cap, later dull red-brown and cracking.

Gilded Bolete
Auireoboletus gentilis (edible)

HABITAT Broadleaved woodland on clay, mainly with oak
OCCURRENCE Autumn; uncommon

CAP 2.5–5cm across; bun-shaped then flatter; sticky; peach to dirty pink
STEM 3–8cm long x 5–10mm thick; narrowing to the pointed base, smooth and sticky; flushed pinkish, yellow at top
FLESH Whitish, pinkish under the cap, lemon yellow above tubes
PORES Small; golden yellow, unchanging
SPORES Ochre-buff
SMELL Pleasant

SIMILAR SPECIES

No similar species – Gilded Bolete is the only bolete species with unchanging, golden yellow pores and a sticky pink cap, found in broadleaved woodland.

Parasitic Bolete
Pseudoboletus parasiticus (edible)

HABITAT On Common Earthball *Scleroderma citrinum*
OCCURRENCE Autumn; occasional

CAP 2–4cm across; bun-shaped then flatter; slightly downy; dirty straw-yellow to mid-brown
STEM 2–4cm long x 4–10mm thick; tapering towards base, often curved; dirty straw-yellow to mid-brown
FLESH Pale lemon yellow, unchanging
PORES Small; lemon yellow, becoming rusty brown
SPORES Olive brown
SMELL Not distinctive

SIMILAR SPECIES

No similar species – only Parasitic Bolete grows on Common Earthball *Scleroderma citrinum* (see page 66).

Orange Birch Bolete
Leccinum versipelle (edible)

HABITAT With birch trees
OCCURRENCE Summer–autumn; occasional

CAP 5–20cm across; bun-shaped to convex;
downy then smooth, slightly sticky when
wet; yellowish brown-orange
STEM 7–20cm long x 15–40mm thick;
whitish to grey, covered in woolly
brownish-black scales
FLESH Whitish, later dark purplish-brown,
finally blackish
PORES Small; pale mouse grey, later ochre
SPORES Walnut brown
SMELL Pleasant

SIMILAR SPECIES

Leccinum aurantiacum (edible)
is similar in size, shape and
colour, but is found with aspen
trees. Stem is whitish covered in
scales that are whitish at first,
then rusty brown later. Flesh is
whitish, turning dark purplish-
brown in cap. Pores are white to
cream, bruising purplish-brown.

Brown Birch Bolete
Leccinum scabrum (edible)

HABITAT With birch trees
OCCURRENCE Summer–autumn; very common

CAP 5–20cm across; bun-shaped to convex;
smooth but sticky when wet; dark to
mid-brown or buff
STEM 7–20cm long x 20–30mm thick;
white to grey, covered in brownish-
black scales
FLESH Whitish, soft and watery
PORES Small; whitish, later pale brown-
buff, bruising ochre
SPORES Walnut brown
SMELL Pleasant

SIMILAR SPECIES

Mottled Bolete *Leccinum
variicolor* (edible), found with
birch trees, is similar in size, but
has a mottled mouse grey to
dark brown cap. Stem is whitish
covered in grey scales, bruising
greenish-yellow. Flesh is pinkish
in cap, blue-green in stem base.
Pores white to cream, bruising
pinkish to purplish-brown.

Slippery Jack
Suillus luteus (edible)

HABITAT With coniferous trees, usually Scots pine
OCCURRENCE Autumn; common

CAP 5–12cm across; convex; very slimy; chestnut brown
STEM 5–10cm long x 20–30mm thick; with a large cream to brownish ring; pale straw-coloured
FLESH White
PORES Round, straw to lemon yellow
SPORES Clay brown to ochre
SMELL Not distinctive

SIMILAR SPECIES

Larch Bolete *Suillus grevillei* (edible), found with larch, also has a ring on the stem, but cap is yellow, flushed rusty brown. **Bovine Bolete** *Suillus bovinus* (edible), found with Scots pine, has a clay-pink slimy cap. Pores are large and angular, olive-buff to ochre. **Weeping Bolete** *Suillus granulatus* (edible), found with coniferous trees, has a chestnut brown, slimy cap. Pores are yellow and exude milky droplets (hence the name).

Old Man of the Woods
Strobilomyces strobilaceus (edible)

HABITAT Broadleaved and coniferous woodland, usually with beech
OCCURRENCE Early autumn; occasional

CAP 5–12cm across; bun-shaped to convex; smoky-grey, later mouse grey to dark grey/black, covered in large, thick, grey scales, some overhanging, giving a ragged edge
STEM 8–12cm long x 10–20mm thick; mouse grey to white above, darker below, covered in large scales
FLESH White, gradually turning coral then brown when cut
PORES Large and angular; white to grey, bruising coral then red
SPORES Violet-black
SMELL Not distinctive

SIMILAR SPECIES

No similar species – Old Man of the Woods is unmistakable with its shaggy, grey cap.

False Chanterelle

Hygrophoropsis aurantiaca (inedible)

HABITAT Coniferous woodland, heathland
OCCURRENCE Late summer–autumn; very common

CAP 2–8cm across; convex to shallowly funnel-shaped; downy; orange-yellow with a paler edge
STEM 3–5cm long x 5–10mm thick; often curved; orange-yellow to orange
FLESH Yellowish to orange
GILLS Running down onto stem, narrow and forked; orange
SPORES White
SMELL Mushroomy

SIMILAR SPECIES

Chanterelle *Cantharellus cibarius*, found in broadleaved and coniferous woodland, often in mossy areas, is fleshier, deep egg-yellow and smells of apricot (see page 57). There are several orange-coloured **milkcap** *Lactarius* species (see page 44), but these exude a milky liquid if cap or gills are broken.

Brown Rollrim

Paxillus involutus (poisonous, possibly deadly)

HABITAT Broadleaved woodland and heathland, usually with birch
OCCURRENCE Summer–autumn; very common

CAP 5–14cm across; convex then shallowly funnel-shaped, the edge remaining inrolled; downy but slimy when wet; ochre to yellowish-brown, becoming rusty brown
STEM 4–8cm long x 8–12mm thick; ochre to yellowish-brown, bruising chestnut
FLESH Pale ochre, darkening when cut
GILLS Running down onto stem, crowded; pale ochre, later more brownish, bruising chestnut
SPORES Brown
SMELL Not distinctive

SIMILAR SPECIES

Some **milkcap** *Lactarius* species look similar, but exude a milky liquid when the gills or cap is broken. **Chanterelle** *Cantherellus cibarius* (see page 57) is smaller and fleshier and smells of apricot.

Chanterelle

Cantharellus cibarius (edible)

HABITAT Broadleaved and coniferous woodland, often in moss
OCCURRENCE Summer–autumn; common

CAP 3–10cm across; flat with an irregular edge, later wavy
and funnel-shaped; pale to deep egg-yellow
STEM 3–8cm long x 5–15mm thick; tapering towards
the base; pale to deep egg-yellow
FLESH Yellowish and watery
GILLS Running down onto stem, thick and fleshy,
vein-like and forked; egg-yellow
SPORES Ochre
SMELL Faintly of apricot

SIMILAR SPECIES

Trumpet Chanterelle
Cantharellus tubaeformis (edible),
found in broadleaved and
coniferous woodland (see page 6),
has brown cap, grey gills and
yellow stem. **False Chanterelle**
Hygrophoropsis aurantiaca
(inedible) is more orange (see
page 56). **Brown Rollrim** *Paxillus
involutus* (poisonous, possibly
deadly) has an ochre cap with
inrolled margin, gills and stem
bruise chestnut (see page 56).

Horn of Plenty

Craterellus cornucopioides (edible)

HABITAT In clusters, in leaf litter in broadleaved
woodland, especially beech
OCCURRENCE Summer–autumn; occasional

CAP 2–8cm across x 3–10cm high; deeply
funnel-shaped, with a flared, rolled-back
mouth; inner surface is dark brown to black,
drying paler; spore-bearing outer surface is
ash grey , smooth then undulating
STEM Short and hollow, merging with cap
FLESH Thin and leathery
GILLS Absent
SPORES White
SMELL Not distinctive

SIMILAR SPECIES

The rare **Sinuous Chanterelle**
Pseudocraterellus undulatus
(edible), found clustered in leaf
litter of broadleaved woodland,
usually with beech, looks like a
paler, miniature version of horn of
plenty. Cap is 1–5cm across,
funnel-shaped and irregularly
lobed, with a streaky greyish-
brown inner surface and a creamy
spore-bearing outer surface.

Wood Hedgehog
Hydnum repandum (edible)

HABITAT Broadleaved and coniferous woodland
OCCURRENCE Late summer–autumn; common

CAP 3–15cm across; flattened-convex, uneven and lumpy, often with a depression; suede-like texture; cream to flesh-coloured
STEM 3.5–7.5cm long x 15–40mm thick; off-centre; white, bruising yellowish near the base
FLESH White, bruising yellowish
SPINES 2–6mm long, running down to stem; whitish to flesh-coloured
SPORES White
SMELL Pleasant

SIMILAR SPECIES

The less common **Terracotta Hedgehog** *Hydnum rufescens* (edible), found in broadleaved and coniferous woodland, is smaller, has a smaller (2–8cm across), orange-brown cap. Spines do not run down to stem.

White Coral
Clavulina coralloides (edible)

HABITAT Broadleaved and coniferous woodland, in troops or small clusters
OCCURRENCE Summer–autumn; common

FRUIT BODY 2.5–8cm high; densely branched tufts (resembling coral), tips often fringed; white to pale cream, greying with age
FLESH White and brittle
SPORES White
SMELL Not distinctive

SIMILAR SPECIES

Wrinkled Club *Clavulina rugosa* (edible) is less branched and does not form dense tufts. Its surface is wrinkled and uneven. **Grey Coral** *Clavulina cinerea* (edible) is grey-lilac and has blunter branches. **Upright Coral** *Ramaria stricta* (inedible), found on stumps and debris in broadleaved woodland and occasionally on coniferous trees, is pale ochre.

Yellow Club
Clavulinopsis helvola (inedible)

HABITAT Open mixed woodland and clearings, solitary or
in small groups
OCCURRENCE Late summer–autumn; common

FRUIT BODY 1–7cm high x 2–4mm thick; club-shaped;
yellow to orange-yellow
FLESH Fibrous; pale yellow
SPORES White to pale yellow
SMELL Not distinctive

SIMILAR SPECIES

Golden Spindles *Clavulinopsis
fusiformis* (inedible), growing in
dense tufts in grassland and
amongst grass on heathland, is
spindle-shaped and bright yellow.
Meadow Coral *Clavulinopsis
corniculata* (edible), found in
grassland and woodland, forms
branched tufts and is more ochre
yellow in colour.

Moor Club
Clavaria argillacea (edible)

HABITAT Heathland
OCCURRENCE Summer–autumn; occasional

FRUIT BODY 3–5cm high x 2–8mm thick; club-shaped;
creamy-yellow to greenish-yellow, deeper coloured
towards the base
FLESH Brittle; pale yellow
SPORES White
SMELL Not distinctive

SIMILAR SPECIES

Smokey Spindles *Clavaria
fumosa* (inedible), is taller
(1.5–12cm) and is found in
grass, forming tufts. It is mouse
grey in colour and spindle-
shaped. **White Spindles**
Clavaria fragilis (inedible), found
in grass, forming dense tufts, is
white and spindle-shaped.

Slender Club
Macrotyphula juncea (inedible)

HABITAT Solitary or in large groups amongst leaf litter in broadleaved woodland
OCCURRENCE Autumn; occasional

FRUIT BODY 3–10cm high x 0.5–2mm thick; very slender and spindle-shaped, with a pointed tip, later slightly blunted; pale ochre with a darker base
FLESH Tough; pale yellowish
SPORES White
SMELL Sour

SIMILAR SPECIES

Pipe Club *Macrotyphula fistulosa* (inedible), occasionally found on twigs and leaf litter in broadleaved woodland, is much taller at 7–30cm (see below).

Pipe Club
Macrotyphula fistulosa (inedible)

HABITAT On twigs and in leaf litter, broadleaved woodland
OCCURRENCE Autumn–early winter; occasional

FRUIT BODY 7–30cm high x 2–8mm thick; slender and spindle-shaped, with a pointed tip, later slightly blunted; dirty yellow to yellowish-brown, darker at the base
FLESH Tough; yellowish
SPORES White
SMELL Not distinctive

SIMILAR SPECIES

Slender Club *Macrotyphula juncea* (inedible), is found on twigs and in leaf litter in damp broadleaved woodland (see above). Although it can appear in large numbers, it is often overlooked, as it is 3–10cm tall, very thin and needle-like.

Yellow Stagshorn
Calocera viscosa (inedible)

HABITAT On stumps and roots of coniferous trees
OCCURRENCE Autumn; common

FRUIT BODY 3–10cm high; branched like anters
(hence the name); deep golden yellow to
orange-yellow, drying more orange
FLESH Tough and gelatinous; pale yellow
SPORES White
SMELL Not distinctive

SIMILAR SPECIES

Meadow Coral *Clavulinopsis corniculata* (edible), also branched, grows in tufts in grassland and woodland, and is more ochre yellow. **Small Stagshorn** *Calocera cornea* (inedible), growing in groups, like yellow spines, on twigs and branches of broadleaved trees, is tiny (to 1cm tall) and unbranched or very rarely forked.

Earthfan
Thelephora terrestris (inedible)

HABITAT Coniferous woodland, heathland
OCCURRENCE Late summer–early winter; common

FRUIT BODY 3–6cm across; fan-shaped, forming large,
clustered groups; upper surface is reddish-brown to
chocolate brown, covered in radiating fibres
becoming paler and fringed along the edge;
lower surface is clay brown and wrinkled
FLESH Fibrous and tough; brown
SPORES Purplish-brown
SMELL Faint and earthy

SIMILAR SPECIES

The rare **Zoned Tooth** *Hydnellum concrescens* (inedible), is found in broadleaved and coniferous woodland, growing in fused clusters. Similar in colour, the underside is quite different, having small pointed teeth. *Thelephora pencillata* (inedible), found on twigs and leaf litter in damp broadleaved and coniferous woodland, is 2–15cm across and is made up of numerous spiky branches forming white rosettes, purplish-brown in the centre.

Oyster Mushroom
Pleurotus ostreacus (edible)

HABITAT In tiered clusters on living, fallen and dead wood of broadleaved trees, especially beech
OCCURRENCE All year; very common

CAP 6–14cm across; shell-shaped, convex then flattened or slightly depressed; creamy-brown or blue-grey
STEM 2–3cm long x 10–20mm thick; off-centre; white
FLESH White
GILLS Running down onto stem; white, later tinged yellowish
SPORES Lilac
SMELL Pleasant

SIMILAR SPECIES

Pale Oyster *Pleurotus palmonarius* (edible), found in tiered clusters on fallen and dead wood of broadleaved trees in the autumn, is similar, but is white to cream in colour. **Branching Oyster** *Pleurotus cornucopiae* (edible), grows in dense, trumpet-shaped clusters on stumps of broadleaved trees, is cream to ochre in colour, and has a distinct stem.

62

Dryad's Saddle
Polyporus squamosus (edible)

HABITAT Parasitic on broadleaved trees
OCCURRENCE Spring to early autumn; very common

BRACKET 5–60cm x 3–5cm across, 5–30mm thick; flat, circular to fan-shaped; ochre-cream, covered in dark brown, concentric scales
STEM 3–10cm long x 10–60mm thick; near the edge or off-centre; dark brown
FLESH Succulent, drying corky; white
PORES Irregular and angular; whitish to ochre-cream
SPORES White
SMELL Mealy

SIMILAR SPECIES

Bay Polypore *Polyporus durus* (inedible), found on dead or living broadleaved trees, is smaller (5–20cm across), bay brown to chestnut in colour (not scaly) and sticky when wet, drying smooth and shiny. Pores are small, circular and white, later cream.

Blushing Bracket
Daedaleopsis confragosa (inedible)

HABITAT Singly or in small tiers on broadleaved trees, especially willows
OCCURRENCE All year; very common

BRACKET 8–22cm x 4–10cm across, 15–30mm thick; semicircular, single or tiered; wrinkled and concentrically ridged; reddish-brown
FLESH Corky; white, later pale brown
PORES Large, elongated to slit-like; whitish, bruising pinkish to reddish if handled
SPORES White
SMELL None

SIMILAR SPECIES

Birch Mazegill *Lenzites betulinus* (inedible), found on broadleaved trees, especially birch, is smaller (3–8cm across), concentrically zoned whitish, tan and brown. The pores are very elongated and look like gills.

Turkeytail
Trametes versicolor (inedible)

HABITAT In tiered clusters on wood of broadleaved trees
OCCURRENCE All year; very common

BRACKET 4–10cm x 3–5cm across, 10–30mm thick; forming overlapping, tiered clusters; velvet-like surface; very variable in colour, concentrically zoned blackish-green, grey-blue, brown and rusty-brow, with a white or cream edge
FLESH Tough and leathery; white
PORES Tiny, circular or angular; white to pale cream
SPORES White
SMELL Not distinctive

SIMILAR SPECIES

Zoned Tooth *Hydnellum concrescens* (inedible), is a rare fungus, found on the ground in broadleaved and coniferous woodland, growing in clusters, often fused together. It is similar in colour and zoning, but the underside is quite different, having small pointed teeth instead of pores.

Chicken of the Woods
Laetiporus sulphureus (edible when young)

HABITAT In tiered clusters on broadleaved trees
OCCURRENCE Spring–autumn; common

BRACKET 10–40cm across; fan-shaped with a
rounded edge, forming large, tiered clusters;
yellow or yellow-orange with a yellow
lower surface, thick and fleshy
FLESH Succulent at first, exuding yellow
liquid if squeezed, later white and
crumbly
PORES Circular to oval; sulphur yellow
SPORES White
SMELL Strong and fungusy

SIMILAR SPECIES

No similar species – Chicken of
the Woods is unmistakable,
with its large size and vibrant
colouring.

Birch Polypore or Razorstrop Fungus
Piptoporus betulinum (inedible)

HABITAT On birch trees
OCCURRENCE All year; very common

BRACKET 10–20cm across, 2–6cm thick; rounded then
hoof-shaped with a rounded edge; smooth and
leathery; whitish, then pale greyish-brown
FLESH Rubbery and leathery (once used to sharpen
knives and razors, hence its alternative name –
razorstrop fungus); white
PORES Tiny, circular; white, then pale grey-brown
SPORES White
SMELL Strong and fungusy

SIMILAR SPECIES

No similar species – Birch
Polypore is unmistakable, as it
is very common and only found
on birch trees.

Conifer Blueing Bracket
Postia caesia (inedible)

HABITAT On dead coniferous trees, especially spruce
OCCURRENCE All year; occasional

BRACKET 1–6cm x 1–4cm across, 3–10mm thick; semicircular, single or in groups; whitish at first, becoming grey-blue with age
FLESH Tough; whitish
PORES Circular; white
SPORES White
SMELL Not distinctive

SIMILAR SPECIES
Blueing Bracket *Postia subcaesia* (inedible) is similar, but is found all year on fallen branches of broadleaved trees in old woodland.

Willow Bracket
Phellinus igniarius (inedible)

HABITAT Parasitic on broadleaved trees, especially willows
OCCURRENCE Spring–late autumn; occasional

BRACKET 10–40cm x 2–8cm across, 5–20cm thick; hoof-shaped with a rounded edge; very hard and woody, concentrically ridged, becoming cracked; rusty brown when young, later grey, then black with the edge remaining rusty brown
FLESH Hard; rusty brown
PORES Circular; cinnamon to maroon
SPORES Dark brown
SMELL Fungusy

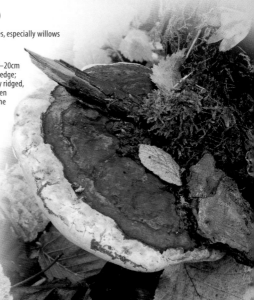

SIMILAR SPECIES
Phellinus nigricans (inedible), a rare species found on living or dead birch, is similar in size and shape, but is zoned whitish, grey and cinnamon with concentric lack grooves. Pores are cinnamon to dark rusty brown.

Common Puffball
Lycoperdon perlatum (edible when young)

HABITAT Broadleaved and coniferous woodland
OCCURRENCE Summer–autumn; very common

FRUIT BODY 2.5–6cm across, 2–5cm high; almost spherical with a distinct stem; white, covered in conical warts that soon brush off, later ochre-brown, skin becomes paper-thin with an opening at the top when mature, through which the spores are released
SPORE MASS White, olive brown when mature
SPORES Olive brown
SMELL Not distinctive

SIMILAR SPECIES

Spiny Puffball *Lycoperdon echinatum* (inedible), found in broadleaved woodland, is brownish and has long spines that converge at the tips. **Stump Puffball** *Lycoperdon pyriforme* (edible), is pear-shaped and grows in large clusters on stumps of broadleaved and coniferous trees. **Giant Puffball** *Calvatia gigantea* (edible), found in grassland and hedgerows, is huge, growing to 50cm across.

Common Earthball
Scleroderma citrinum (inedible)

HABITAT With broadleaved trees in woodland, especially on sandy soils, and heathland
OCCURRENCE Summer–autumn; very common

FRUIT BODY 2–10cm across, 4cm high; spherical with a short stem with cord-like threads; yellow to ochre-brown, thick and tough skin is covered in tough, coarse scales and splits open when mature, through which the spores are released
SPORE MASS Purplish-black, dark olive brown when mature
SPORES Brown
SMELL Strong and unpleasant

SIMILAR SPECIES

Scaly Earthball *Scleroderma verrucosum* (inedible), found on sandy soil in woodland and heathland. The flattened-round fruit body tapers to a long, stem-like base and is pale brown, covered in small brown scales.

Collared Earthstar
Geastrum triplex (inedible)

HABITAT In leaf litter in broadleaved woodland, occasionally in
needle litter in coniferous woodland
OCCURRENCE Late summer–autumn; occasional
FRUIT BODY 3–5cm across, 4cm high; bulb-shaped at first,
outer skin splitting into 4–8 pointed rays, 5–10cm across,
revealing the inner skin, surrounded by a collar; pinkish-
brown on rays, pale grey-brown on inner skin that becomes
paper-thin with an opening at the top when mature,
through which the spores are released
SPORES Dark brown
SMELL Not distinctive

SIMILAR SPECIES

Geastrum rufescens (inedible), found in
broadleaved woodland, lacks the collar
surrounding the sack-like inner skin, as
does the uncommon *Geastrum coronatum*,
found in broadleaved and coniferous
woodland.

Common Bird's Nest
Crucibulum laeve (inedible)

HABITAT In groups on wood, twigs and other organic debris
OCCURRENCE Autumn–early spring; common
FRUIT BODY 4–8mm across, 3–7mm high; spherical and
covered by a yellowish skin at first, then deeply cup-shaped
('nest'-like) with a yellowish-brown outer surface and a
dirty silvery-grey inner surface
SPORE CONTAINERS Lens-shaped 'eggs' attached to 'nest' by
short threads; greyish-white
SPORES White to yellowish
SMELL Not distinctive

SIMILAR SPECIES

Field Bird's Nest *Cyathus olla* (inedible),
found on soil, twigs and other organic
debris, is more silvery-grey. **Fluted Bird's
Nest** *Cyathus striatus* (inedible), found on
cones, stumps, twigs and bark mulch, has a
hairy outer surface and a grooved inner
surface to the 'nest'.

Stinkhorn
Phallus impudicus (the egg stage is edible)

HABITAT Woodland and gardens, associated with rotting wood which may be buried
OCCURRENCE Summer–autumn; very common

FRUIT BODY Egg-like at first (3–6cm across), half buried in soil, with a gelatinous layer beneath the white skin; phallic-shaped white stem-like structure erupts from egg, expanding to 10–25cm, bell-shaped head is covered in dark olive-brown slime that contains the spores; the spores are dispersed by flies that are attracted by the offensive smell of the slime
SPORES Pale yellow
SMELL Strong and offensive, like rotting meat

SIMILAR SPECIES

Dog Stinkhorn *Mutinus caninus* (inedible), found in leaf litter in woodland, is similar but smaller and thinner. The head is orange-red and covered in dark olive-brown slime. Spores are dispersed in a similar fashion to Stinkhorn.

Jelly Ear
Auricularia auricula-judae (edible)

HABITAT On branches of broadleaved trees, especially elder
OCCURRENCE All year; very common

FRUIT BODY 3–8cm across; ear-shaped; outer surface is brown with minute downy hairs, inner surface is grey-brown and wrinkled
FLESH Gelatinous
SPORES White
SMELL Not distinctive

SIMILAR SPECIES

Tripe Fungus *Auricularia mesenterica* (inedible), found on stumps and logs of broadleaved trees, all-year round, is similar in size, disc-shaped and grows in tiered, gelatinous brackets. The upper surface is hairy and concentrically zoned grey to grey-brown, the lower surface is wrinkled and reddish-purple to dark purple.

White Saddle
Helvella crispa (inedible)

HABITAT Path sides in damp, broadleaved woodland
OCCURRENCE Late summer–autumn; common

CAP 2–5cm high; convoluted saddle-shaped with irregular lobes; whitish
STEM 2–6cm long x 10–20mm thick; hollow and deeply furrowed; white
SPORES White
SMELL Not distinctive

SIMILAR SPECIES

Elfin Saddle *Helvella lacunosa* (inedible), found in mixed woodland, is similar in size and shape, but is grey to blackish in colour. **Elastic Saddle** *Helvella elastica* (inedible), found in open woodland, is smaller, and has a irregularly lobed, saddle-shaped cap, grey-brown to yellowish-brown in colour. The whitish stem is not furrowed.

Morel
Morchella esculenta (edible)

HABITAT Open scrub and woodland (often on chalk or limestone), waste ground, gardens
OCCURRENCE Late spring; uncommon

CAP 4–15cm high; round to bluntly conical, honeycomb-like and brittle; pale yellowish-brown, becoming dark reddish-brown
STEM 2–6cm long x 10–15mm thick; hollow, slightly swollen at base; whitish to cream
SPORES Cream
SMELL Not distinctive

SIMILAR SPECIES

False Morel *Gyromitra esculenta* (**deadly poisonous** when raw), found with conifers (usually pine), during the spring, is similar but the convoluted cap is reddish-brown. **Semifree Morel** *Morchella semilibera* (inedible), also found in scrub and woodland during the spring, is smaller with a conical, dark olive-brown, honeycomb-like head.

Scarlet Elfcup
Sarcoscypha austriaca (inedible)

HABITAT In small groups on dead wood and twigs of broadleaved trees
OCCURRENCE Late winter–spring; occasional

CUP 1–5cm across; cup-shaped with a short stem; inner surface bright scarlet, outer surface whitish to pale pink, covered in white, matted hairs
SPORES White
SMELL Not distinctive

SIMILAR SPECIES

Orange Peel Fungus *Aleuria aurantia* (edible), found in groups on bare soil or amongst grass, is bright orange. **Common Eyelash** *Scutellinia scutellata* (inedible), found on damp soil or rotten wood, is only 2–10mm across. The inner surface is orange-red, and is lined with tiny black hairs (hence the name 'eyelash').

Jellybaby
Leotia luibrica (inedible)

HABITAT Damp broadleaved woodland, by paths and under bracken
OCCURRENCE Late summer–autumn; common

HEAD 1–2cm across; convex, edge rolled under, irregularly lobed, slightly sticky; olive-ochre to yellow ochre
STEM 1–5cm long x 3–8mm thick; tapering towards base; yellow ochre
SPORES White
SMELL Not distinctive

SIMILAR SPECIES

Trumpet Chanterelle *Cantharellus tubaeformis* (edible), found in broadleaved and coniferous woodland (see page 6), is larger, although small specimens can look similar. It has a brown cap, grey gills and yellow stem.

King Alfred's Cakes
Daldinia concentrica (inedible)

HABITAT In groups, on fallen or standing dead wood of broadleaved trees, mainly ash and birch

OCCURRENCE All year; very common

FRUIT BODY 2–10cm across; ball-shaped (hence other common name – Cramp Balls), hard and light; pinkish-brown to rusty brown, soon becoming burnt black (hence the name) and shiny

FLESH Concentrically zoned, silver-grey and black

SPORES Black

SMELL Not distinctive

SIMILAR SPECIES

Dead Man's Fingers *Xylaria polymorpha* (inedible), found all-year round in groups on stumps of broadleaved trees, usually beech, is black and finger-like. Flesh is tough, white. **Black Bulgar** *Bulgaria inquinans* (inedible), found in the autumn on dead wood of broadleaved trees, usually oak, is black and rubbery, round with a flattened top.

Candlesnuff Fungus
Xylaria hypoxylon (inedible)

HABITAT In groups, on dead wood

OCCURRENCE All year; very common

FRUIT BODY 1–6cm high; cylindrical and stick-like, becoming flattened and branched like antlers (hence other common name – Stag's Horn); white and powdery, black and hairy at base

FLESH White and tough

SPORES Black

SMELL Not distinctive

SIMILAR SPECIES

Dead Man's Fingers *Xylaria polymorpha* (inedible), found on stumps of broadleaved trees, usually beech, is black and finger-like.

Species index

72